INTER

MW00889389

BASKETBALL

TRIVIA BOOK

550 Entertaining Basketball Trivia Questions and
Answers Plus Interesting Facts and Basketball
Word Search Puzzles

CHUKU MICHAEL

Copyright © 2024 by Chuku Michael
ALL RIGHTS RESERVED

No part of this book may be reproduced, distributed, or transmitted in any form or by any means, including photocopying, recording, or other electronic or mechanical methods, without the prior written permission of the author, except in the case of brief quotations embodied in critical reviews and certain other noncommercial uses permitted by copyright law.

Note from the Author

As this book ages, answers to some questions that are date-related and that are correct as of September 2024, may likely change. However, such questions are relatively small in number.

Disclaimer

The data and information presented in this book are for informational purposes only. The author has made every effort to ensure the accuracy of the information contained within but cannot be held liable for any errors, omissions, losses, or damages that may arise from its use.
Please contact info@funsided.com if you discover an error or omission in this book.

Table Of Contents

Introduction

Ever found yourself in a conversation about basketball, wanting to throw in an amazing fact, or asking a question that stumps everyone? This book is here to make you the go-to basketball trivia master.

Whether you're hanging out with friends, waiting for a game to start, bored on a road trip, or looking for something fun to do on a quiet afternoon, this Interesting Basketball Trivia and Fact Book is packed with surprises and challenges for every fan.

Not only does this book make trivia fun, but it also reveals the quirks and historic milestones of the game. Did you know the San Francisco Warriors drafted a high school girl in 1969, making her one of the most unusual NBA picks ever?

Or that Rasheed Wallace set an unbelievable record with 41 technical fouls in a single season? And what about the first slam dunk ever recorded? It happened in 1936 and was performed by Joe Fortenberry—a Texan who set the stage for the game's most iconic move.

With intriguing questions like, "Which NBA team holds the record for the longest winning streak?" and "What type of foul is called when a player kicks the basketball?" you'll find trivia that ranges from quirky to challenging. This book is loaded with quick facts, memorable questions, and thought-provoking trivia that'll keep you on your toes.

In addition to all the trivia and fun facts, this book includes basketball-themed word search puzzles that add another level of challenge. These puzzles are crafted around basketball slang, iconic players, and essential

Table Of Contents

Introduction

Ever found yourself in a conversation about basketball, wanting to throw in an amazing fact, or asking a question that stumps everyone? This book is here to make you the go-to basketball trivia master.

Whether you're hanging out with friends, waiting for a game to start, bored on a road trip, or looking for something fun to do on a quiet afternoon, this Interesting Basketball Trivia and Fact Book is packed with surprises and challenges for every fan.

Not only does this book make trivia fun, but it also reveals the quirks and historic milestones of the game. Did you know the San Francisco Warriors drafted a high school girl in 1969, making her one of the most unusual NBA picks ever?

Or that Rasheed Wallace set an unbelievable record with 41 technical fouls in a single season? And what about the first slam dunk ever recorded? It happened in 1936 and was performed by Joe Fortenberry—a Texan who set the stage for the game's most iconic move.

With intriguing questions like, "Which NBA team holds the record for the longest winning streak?" and "What type of foul is called when a player kicks the basketball?" you'll find trivia that ranges from quirky to challenging. This book is loaded with quick facts, memorable questions, and thought-provoking trivia that'll keep you on your toes.

In addition to all the trivia and fun facts, this book includes basketball-themed word search puzzles that add another level of challenge. These puzzles are crafted around basketball slang, iconic players, and essential terms, helping you dive even deeper into the language and culture of basketball.

Whether you're a lifelong fan of basketball or new to the game, this book will deepen your appreciation of the game and keep you entertained. So, dive in, and let's explore the surprising, fun, and unforgettable world of basketball together!

Multiple Choice Questions

1. In what year was the first-ever NBA game played between the New York Knicks and the Toronto Huskies?
A. 1950
B. 1948
C. 1946

2. Who is the youngest player to ever win the NBA MVP award at age 22?
A. LeBron James
B. Derrick Rose
C. Magic Johnson

3. What unique shot did Kareem Abdul-Jabbar create in his NBA career?
A. Hook shot
B. Fadeaway
C. Skyhook

4. Which NBA player holds the record for most double-doubles in a season as of 2024?
A. Giannis Antetokounmpo
B. Domantas Sabonis
C. Nikola Jokic

5. Which player holds the record for most career double-doubles in the NBA with 968 in 2024?
A. Wilt Chamberlain
B. Karl Malone
C. Tim Duncan

6. Nikola Jokic became the first center since the 1970s to win MVP. In which season did he first win this award?
A. 2021-22
B. 2019-20
C. 2020-21

7. How many NBA championships did Bill Russell win in his 13-year NBA career?
A. 12
B. 11
C. 10

8. Which team knocked the Boston Celtics out of the 2018 NBA playoffs?
A. Philadelphia 76ers
B. Milwaukee Bucks
C. Cleveland Cavaliers

9. Which team won the NBA Championship in 2023?
A. Denver Nuggets
B. Golden State Warriors
C. Milwaukee Bucks

10. What was the National Basketball Association (NBA) originally called?
A. The Basketball Association of America
B. American Basketball League
C. National Basketball League

11. What is Dr. J's original name?
A. Julius Erving
B. Michael Jordan
C. Charles Barkley

12. Which year was Michael Jordan drafted into the NBA?

A. 1983

B. 1984

C. 1985

13. Which NBA team is called the "Red Oxen" in China?

A. Houston Rockets

B. Los Angeles Lakers

C. Chicago Bulls

14. Which famous basketball player's name means "little warrior"?

A. Allen Iverson

B. Shaquille O'Neal

C. Kobe Bryant

15. What shot technique did Paul Arizin popularize in the NBA?

A. Hook shot

B. Running jump shot

C. Fadeaway

16. What nickname did Charles Barkley earn for his powerful rebounding ability despite being considered undersized?

A. Air Barkley

B. The Round Mound of Rebound

C. Sir Charles

17. How many players should be on the court for one team in a basketball game?

A. 6

B. 4

C. 5

18. Which player drafted out of St. John's in 1999 is known for his excellent defense at the forward position?
A. Latrell Sprewell
B. Metta World Peace (Ron Artest)
C. John Starks

19. Which jersey number did Tim Duncan wear for the 2007 San Antonio Spurs?
A. 21
B. 22
C. 25

20. Is a dunk classified as a variety of shot in basketball?
A. Yes
B. No

21. Which year was the first NBA All-Star Game played?
A. 1947
B. 1955
C. 1951

22. In which film did Kevin Durant appear in 2012?
A. Thunderstruck
B. Space Jam 2
C. Uncle Drew

23. Who was the first African-American to play in an NBA game?
A. Chuck Cooper
B. Bill Russell
C. Earl Lloyd

24. Who was the first player to score 100 points in an NBA game?
A. Michael Jordan

B. Wilt Chamberlain

C. Kobe Bryant

25. How many personal fouls will cause a player to be ejected from an NBA game?

A. 5 in 40-minute games or 6 in 48-minute games

B. 4 in 40-minute games or 5 in 48-minute games

C. 6 in all games

26. What is the standard height of an NBA basketball hoop?

A. 9 feet

B. 11 feet

C. 10 feet

27. Rick Barry is well-known for using what unique shooting technique for free throws?

A. Jump shot free throw

B. One-handed free throw

C. Underhand free throw

28. After inbounding/throw-in, how many seconds does a team have to move the ball past half-court?

A. 5 seconds

B. 10 seconds

C. 15 seconds

29. What is it called in basketball if a player interferes with a ball's downward trajectory after it has been shot?

A. Goaltending

B. Blocking

C. Charging

30. Which player led the league in blocks per game in the 2013-14 season?

A. Dwight Howard

B. Anthony Davis

C. Serge Ibaka

31. Which player won eight championships with the Boston Celtics and was drafted in 1956?

A. Bill Russell

B. Tom Heinsohn

C. Sam Jones

32. What is the name of the penalty called for illegal contact?

A. Double foul

B. Technical foul

C. Personal foul

33. Who won the 2016 NBA All-Star 3-Point Contest?

A. Klay Thompson

B. Stephen Curry

C. Kyrie Irving

34. Which team originally drafted Kobe Bryant?

A. Charlotte Hornets

B. Los Angeles Lakers

C. Philadelphia 76ers

35. When a player fails to dribble while moving, what is this violation called in basketball?

A. Double dribble

B. Carrying

C. Traveling

36. Paul George changed his jersey number from 24 to what?

A. 23

B. 13

C. 14

37. Kirk Hinrich was traded to which team in February 2016?

A. Atlanta Hawks

B. Washington Wizards

C. Chicago Bulls

38. Which NBA star hosted Saturday Night Live in 2018?

A. Kevin Durant

B. LeBron James

C. Charles Barkley

39. How many parts does a standard basketball hoop have?

A. One

B. Three

C. Two

40. How many substitutions are allowed in basketball?

A. 5

B. 10

C. Unlimited

41. Which member of Michigan's Fab Five spent two seasons with Denver and then moved to the Indiana Pacers?

A. Juwan Howard

B. Jalen Rose

C. Chris Webber

42. What is the diameter of a basketball?

A. 24 cm

B. 22 cm

C. 26 cm

43. Which team did Kevin Love spend the first six years of his NBA career with?
A. Los Angeles Lakers
B. Cleveland Cavaliers
C. Minnesota Timberwolves

44. Rick Fox was born in which country?
A. Canada
B. Jamaica
C. United States

45. Who had the most assists per game in the 2022-2023 NBA season?
A. Trae Young
B. Chris Paul
C. James Harden

46. Hakeem Olajuwon played for which NBA team in his last season?
A. Houston Rockets
B. Toronto Raptors
C. New York Knicks

47. Every NBA game begins with two players standing on either side of a referee. What is this called?
A. Tip-off
B. Toss-up
C. Jump ball

48. What is Hakeem Olajuwon's nickname?
A. The Admiral
B. Big O
C. The Dream

49. How long is a quarter in basketball?

A. 10 minutes

B. 12 minutes

C. 15 minutes

50. Doc Rivers coached which team at the start of the 1999 season?

A. Boston Celtics

B. Orlando Magic

C. Los Angeles Clippers

51. When a player touches a ball twice before it hits the ground and without an opposing player touching it, what rule does the player break?

A. Dribbling violation

B. Traveling

C. Double dribble

52. Who was the shortest player ever to win the Slam Dunk contest?

A. Nate Robinson

B. Anthony 'Spud' Webb (5'7")

C. Muggsy Bogues

53. The tallest and strongest player mostly covers which key position in basketball?

A. Shooting guard

B. Power forward

C. Center

54. What is Michael Jordan's middle name?

A. Jeffrey

B. David

C. Andrew

55. Which NBA team has made the most appearances in the finals?

A. Los Angeles Lakers

B. Boston Celtics

C. Chicago Bulls

56. What is the name of the Canadian-American teacher who invented basketball?

A. James Naismith

B. George Mikan

C. John Wooden

57. Known as "The Houdini of the Hardwood," Bob Cousy played most of his career with which NBA team?

A. New York Knicks

B. Boston Celtics

C. Philadelphia 76ers

58. The most popular basketball league in the world is?

A. NBA

B. NCAA

C. Euro League

59. In 2015, which team sent out four players to the All-Star Game?

A. Golden State Warriors

B. Atlanta Hawks

C. Cleveland Cavaliers

60. The primary position in basketball abbreviated as PF is?

A. Point Forward

B. Power Forward

C. Post Forward

61. Which year was the NBA founded?

A. 1947

B. 1948

C. 1946

62. Who was the first player-coach in the NBA?

A. Bill Russell

B. Ed Sadowski

C. Lenny Wilkens

63. Who was the star player in the Houston Rockets' title run in 1994?

A. Sam Cassell

B. Hakeem Olajuwon

C. Clyde Drexler

64. In 1998, Steve Nash was traded to which team?

A. Dallas Mavericks

B. Phoenix Suns

C. Sacramento Kings

65. What is the total number of teams in the NBA?

A. 28

B. 32

C. 30

66. Billy Cunningham earned what nickname due to his athleticism and tenacity on the court?

A. Kangaroo Kid

B. Rabbit

C. Flying Bill

67. Detroit Pistons and _____ team participated in the 2004 "Malice at the Palace."

A. Chicago Bulls

B. Indiana Pacers

C. New York Knicks

68. Dan Majerle's nickname is?
A. The Hammer
B. Thunder Dan
C. Captain Marvel

69. Dave DeBusschere played in the NBA and was also a pitcher for which MLB team?
A. Chicago White Sox
B. New York Yankees
C. Detroit Tigers

70. Which NBA team won the 2018 championship?
A. Cleveland Cavaliers
B. Toronto Raptors
C. Golden State Warriors

71. How many points does a successful shot beyond the three arcs at 6.75 meters bring?
A. 3 points
B. 2 points
C. 1 point

72. Which team drafted Jermaine O'Neal in 1996?
A. Indiana Pacers
B. Portland Trail Blazers
C. Miami Heat

73. Pete Maravich died playing basketball.
A. True
B. False

74. Which NBA team has the most championships as of the 2023-2024 NBA season?

A. Boston Celtics

B. Los Angeles Lakers

C. Chicago Bulls

75. In what year did Clyde Drexler win his only NBA Championship with the Houston Rockets?

A. 1994

B. 1995

C. 1996

76. Which year did the three-point shot get introduced in the NBA?

A. 1981

B. 1979

C. 1975

77. Which NBA player is nicknamed "The Mailman"?

A. Shaquille O'Neal

B. Charles Barkley

C. Karl Malone

78. Which NBA team has the most finals appearances without a championship?

A. The Phoenix Suns

B. Utah Jazz

C. Orlando Magic

79. Jay-Z sold his ownership share in the Brooklyn Nets in which year?

A. 2013

B. 2014

C. 2015

80. John Wall played mainly in which position?
A. Shooting guard
B. Point guard
C. Small forward

81. Which NBA franchise has the most finals losses?
A. Los Angeles Lakers
B. Boston Celtics
C. New York Knicks

82. Which NBA legend was known as "The Admiral"?
A. David Robinson
B. Tim Duncan
C. Patrick Ewing

83. In the 2018 NBA Draft, who was taken first overall?
A. Luka Dončić
B. DeAndre Ayton
C. Marvin Bagley III

84. What is the time limit for a coach's timeout request?
A. 100 seconds
B. 90 seconds
C. 120 seconds

85. Which NBA player has played the most NBA playoff games without a finals appearance?
A. Charles Barkley
B. Karl Malone
C. Chris Paul

86. Who is the Los Angeles Lakers' all-time leading scorer?
A. Kareem Abdul-Jabbar

B. Kobe Bryant

C. LeBron James

87. Who is the Miami Heat's all-time leading scorer?

A. LeBron James

B. Dwyane Wade

C. Alonzo Mourning

88. How many referees are used in an NBA game?

A. 2

B. 3

C. 4

89. Which NBA player has the most NBA Finals appearances?

A. Michael Jordan

B. Kareem Abdul-Jabbar

C. Bill Russell

90. Hakeem Olajuwon had a quadruple-double.

A. True

B. False

91. Who invented the shot clock?

A. James Naismith

B. Danny Biasone

C. Chuck Cooper

92. How many points is a free throw worth?

A. 2

B. 3

C. 1

93. Hubie Brown was a coach for Atlanta.

A. True

B. False

94. NBA officials started in?

A. 1946

B. 1948

C. 1950

95. Who was the 2015 dunk contest winner?

A. Zach LaVine

B. Aaron Gordon

C. Giannis Antetokounmpo

96. Pau Gasol is the older brother of who?

A. Marc Gasol

B. Rudy Fernandez

C. Ricky Rubio

97. Who holds the record for most Slam Dunk Contest wins?

A. Michael Jordan

B. Vince Carter

C. Nate Robinson

98. In the 2000s, how many titles did the Minneapolis Lakers win?

A. 6 titles

B. 5 titles

C. 4 titles

99. LeBron James is often called by which nickname?

A. The King

B. King James

C. The Chosen One

100. In the U.S., the basketball governing body is called?
A. FIBA USA
B. USA Basketball (USAB)
C. American Basketball Association

101. How many NBA Finals did Kobe Bryant play in his career?
A. 5
B. 7
C. 6

102. Who was famously known for saying, "I'm not a role model" in a Nike ad?
A. LeBron James
B. Charles Barkley
C. Michael Jordan

103. Which NBA team holds the record for the longest consecutive NBA Finals appearances?
A. Chicago Bulls
B. Los Angeles Lakers
C. Boston Celtics

104. The NBA logo featuring the silhouette of Jerry West officially debuted in which year?
A. 1969
B. 1972
C. 1971

105. The first African-American to be signed by an NBA team was?
A. Harold Hunter
B. Nat "Sweetwater" Clifton
C. Earl Lloyd

106. Which team selected Elfrid Payton and then traded him to the Orlando Magic?
A. Philadelphia 76ers
B. San Antonio Spurs
C. Los Angeles Lakers

107. Carmelo Anthony represented which team in the 2011 All-Star game?
A. Denver Nuggets
B. New York Knicks
C. Miami Heat

108. Which player officially broke the NBA color barrier?
A. Wataru Misaka
B. Chuck Cooper
C. Don Barksdale

109. Steve Nash was born in which country?
A. Canada
B. South Africa
C. Australia

110. Who won the NBA Sixth Man of the Year award in 2011?
A. Jamal Crawford
B. Lamar Odom
C. J.R. Smith

111. Which NBA player was awarded the Double Helix Medal for raising awareness of cancer research?
A. Magic Johnson
B. Kareem Abdul-Jabbar
C. Charles Barkley

112. The Los Angeles Clippers earned which nickname during Chris Paul's debut season?
A. Showtime Clippers
B. Lob City
C. Clipper Nation

113. Which NBA player trained under Bruce Lee?
A. Wilt Chamberlain
B. Kareem Abdul-Jabbar
C. Kobe Bryant

114. Which NBA team has the most playoff appearances?
A. Los Angeles Lakers
B. Boston Celtics
C. Philadelphia 76ers

115. Arvydas Sabonis was originally from which country?
A. Russia
B. Lithuania
C. Latvia

116. Which player has played the most games in Los Angeles Lakers history?
A. Magic Johnson
B. Kobe Bryant
C. Kareem Abdul-Jabbar

117. Who is the only player to win the NBA MVP award as a rookie?
A. Larry Bird
B. Wes Unseld
C. Wilt Chamberlain

118. George Yardley played for which team in the 1957-58 season?

A. Philadelphia Warriors

B. Detroit Falcons

C. Los Angeles Lakers

119. Alvin Robertson had a quadruple-double.

A. True

B. False

120. Since the first NBA Finals in 1950, how many Finals have ended in a
  4-0 sweep?

A. 7

B. 9

C. 10

121. What is Kenny Walker's nickname?

A. The Flash

B. Sky

C. Lightning

122. What is the oldest NBA team without a title?

A. Phoenix Suns

B. Denver Nuggets

C. Utah Jazz

123. In which year's draft was LaMarcus Aldridge selected second overall?

A. 2006

B. 2007

C. 2005

124. Paul Pierce was once stabbed in the face, neck, and back.

A. True

B. False

125. Pau Gasol went to which school before playing professional basketball?

A. Medical School

B. High School

C. Community College

126. Who was the Washington Wizards' second pick in the 2011 NBA draft?

A. Kemba Walker

B. Chris Singleton

C. Kawhi Leonard

127. Who won the NBA MVP award in 2011?

A. Derrick Rose

B. LeBron James

C. Kevin Durant

128. Which NBA team first signed an African American player?

A. New York Knicks

B. Washington Capitols

C. Boston Celtics

129. Which NBA team has the longest winning streak in NBA history?

A. Los Angeles Lakers

B. Golden State Warriors

C. Miami Heat

130. The Naismith Memorial Basketball Hall of Fame is located where?

A. Springfield, Massachusetts

B. New York City, New York

C. Chicago, Illinois

131. Michael Jordan's career high in scoring was?

A. 69 points

B. 64 points

C. 70 points

132. The main sponsor of the 2016 All-Star 3-Point Contest was?

A. Foot Locker

B. Gatorade

C. Nike

133. The NBA team Golden State Warriors is based where?

A. Oakland

B. San Francisco

C. San Diego

134. Which NBA team drafted Derrick Favors third overall in 2010?

A. New Jersey Nets

B. Utah Jazz

C. Denver Nuggets

135. Who is the Chicago Bulls' all-time leading scorer?

A. Scottie Pippen

B. Michael Jordan

C. Derrick Rose

136. The player who came second in the 2015 All-Star Dunk Contest was?

A. Zach LaVine

B. Victor Oladipo

C. Aaron Gordon

137. The first player to score 2,000 points in a season was?

A. George Yardley

B. Wilt Chamberlain

C. Bill Russell

138. The Nike Air Jordan was first released in which year?

A. 1984

B. 1985

C. 1983

139. Who holds the record for most assists in New York Knicks history?

A. Clyde Frazier

B. Walt Frazier

C. Mark Jackson

140. Most basketball courts are constructed with what type of wood?

A. Oak

B. Maple

C. Pine

141. Who won the Skills Challenge in the 2018 All-Stars game?

A. Joel Embiid

B. Spencer Dinwiddie

C. Jayson Tatum

142. Who has the most assists in a single NBA game?

A. Scott Skiles

B. John Stockton

C. Magic Johnson

143. Who is the youngest player to win an NBA championship?

A. Kobe Bryant

B. Magic Johnson

C. Darko Milicic

144. Luis Scola won a gold medal with his country in 2004.

A. True

B. False

145. The 2018 NBA Draft took place where?
A. New York
B. Brooklyn
C. Las Vegas

146. Who was the oldest NBA player?
A. Vince Carter
B. Nat Hickey
C. Robert Parish

147. When did Flip Saunders die?
A. 2015
B. 2016
C. 2014

148. The shortest player in NBA history is?
A. Tyrone Bogues
B. Earl Boykins
C. Spud Webb

149. Which team did Dwyane Wade spend most of his career with?
A. Miami Heat
B. Chicago Bulls
C. Cleveland Cavaliers

150. Patrick Ewing spent the majority of his career with which NBA team?
A. Orlando Magic
B. New York Knicks
C. Seattle SuperSonics

151. How old was Derrick Rose when he won the 2011 MVP award?

A. 23

B. 21

C. 22

152. How many NBA games did Robert Parish appear in?

A. 1200

B. 1611

C. 1400

153. Which NBA team drafted Jordan Hill 8th overall in 2009?

A. Los Angeles Lakers

B. Golden State Warriors

C. New York Knicks

154. Which player won the NBA MVP award in the 2010-11 season?

A. LeBron James

B. Derrick Rose

C. Kevin Durant

155. Walt Frazier's flashy style off the court earned him what nickname?

A. Magic

B. Clyde

C. Pistol

156. Which player led all rookies in blocks during the 2009-10 season?

A. Serge Ibaka

B. DeMarcus Cousins

C. Greg Monroe

157. How many times did Derrick Rose tear his ACL in the 2010-11 season?

A. Once

B. Two times

C. Three times

158. Who has the most assist titles in NBA history?

A. John Stockton

B. Steve Nash

C. Magic Johnson

159. Which player has scored the most points for the Knicks in a game?

A. Carmelo Anthony

B. Bernard King

C. Patrick Ewing

160. Who is the tallest basketball player?

A. Yao Ming

B. Manute Bol

C. Olivier Rioux

161. What NBA player has the most dunks of all time?

A. LeBron James

B. Shaquille O'Neal

C. Dwight Howard

162. How many games did Golden State play to defeat Cleveland in the 2018 NBA Finals?

A. 4 games

B. 5 games

C. 6 games

163. Who has the most steal titles in NBA history?

A. Michael Jordan

B. John Stockton

C. Allen Iverson

164. The first NBA championship was won by which team?

A. New York Knicks

B. Philadelphia Warriors

C. Chicago Stags

165. Michael Jordan's signature shoe was first released in which year?

A. 1985

B. 1983

C. 1984

166. Who won the slam dunk contest at the 2018 NBA All-Star weekend?

A. Zach LaVine

B. Donovan Mitchell

C. Aaron Gordon

167. Who was known as "Chocolate Thunder"?

A. Darryl Dawkins

B. Wilt Chamberlain

C. Karl Malone

168. The first All-Star Game MVP was?

A. Bob Cousy

B. Ed Macauley

C. Bill Russell

169. Michael Jordan was born where?

A. Chicago

B. Brooklyn

C. Wilmington

170. The player with the most steals in a single season is?

A. Michael Jordan

B. Alvin Robertson

C. Scottie Pippen

171. The first player to win multiple NBA Finals MVP awards was?

A. Magic Johnson

B. Willis Reed

C. Kareem Abdul-Jabbar

172. Which NBA player has the most blocks in history?

A. Dikembe Mutombo

B. Hakeem Olajuwon

C. David Robinson

173. Willis Reed won his first MVP award in which year?

A. 1971

B. 1970

C. 1969

174. Which player has the most triple-doubles in NBA history?

A. LeBron James

B. Russell Westbrook

C. Oscar Robertson

175. Yao Ming is originally from which country?

A. Japan

B. China

C. South Korea

176. The team with the worst record in a single NBA season is?

A. Philadelphia 76ers

B. Charlotte Bobcats

C. New York Knicks

177. Which NBA Finals did Kyrie Irving miss due to a knee injury?
A. 2016 Finals
B. 2015 Finals
C. 2017 Finals

178. Which team was Kyrie Irving playing for in 2015?
A. Boston Celtics
B. Cleveland Cavaliers
C. Brooklyn Nets

179. In which season did the Charlotte Bobcats have their worst record?
A. 2012-13 season
B. 2011-12 season
C. 2010-11 season

180. In the 2012 NBA Draft, which team selected Anthony Davis?
A. New Orleans Hornets
B. Washington Wizards
C. Sacramento Kings

181. Which team has won the most consecutive NBA titles?
A. Boston Celtics
B. Los Angeles Lakers
C. Chicago Bulls

182. The Splash Brothers include Stephen Curry and which other player?
A. Klay Thompson
B. Kevin Durant
C. Draymond Green

183. Who holds the record for 30 assists in a single game?
A. Magic Johnson
B. Scott Skiles

C. John Stockton

184. How many consecutive NBA titles have the Boston Celtics won?
A. 7
B. 9
C. 8

185. How many games did Jonny Flynn start in his rookie season?
A. 85
B. 81
C. 82

186. Which team blew a 3-1 lead in the 2016 NBA Finals?
A. Cleveland Cavaliers
B. Golden State Warriors
C. Oklahoma City Thunder

187. Who has the most assists in Golden State Warriors history?
A. Rick Barry
B. Stephen Curry
C. Wilt Chamberlain

188. The first player to win the NBA Finals MVP on a losing team was?
A. Jerry West
B. Kareem Abdul-Jabbar
C. Elgin Baylor

189. Who won the 2015-16 MVP award?
A. LeBron James
B. Stephen Curry
C. Kevin Durant

190. How many seconds does a team have to take a shot that hits the rim in basketball?

A. 24 seconds

B. 30 seconds

C. 28 seconds

191. Who won the MVP of the 2019 NBA Finals?

A. Kawhi Leonard

B. Kevin Durant

C. Stephen Curry

192. The Houston Rockets' head coach in 2007 was?

A. Mike D'Antoni

B. Rick Adelman

C. Jeff Van Gundy

193. The first NBA team to win three consecutive championships was?

A. Los Angeles Lakers

B. Chicago Bulls

C. Boston Celtics

194. Which team was Kevin Durant playing for during the 2019 NBA Finals?

A. Brooklyn Nets

B. Golden State Warriors

C. Oklahoma City Thunder

195. Which team was Jerry West playing for when he won the Finals MVP on a losing team?

A. Los Angeles Lakers

B. Boston Celtics

C. Philadelphia 76ers

196. James Harden made how many 3-pointers in the 2016 All-Star Game?
A. 5 three-pointers
B. 6 three-pointers
C. 7 three-pointers

197. The first team to win the NBA Finals was?
A. Philadelphia Warriors
B. Baltimore Bullets
C. Chicago Stags

198. The "Shot Heard Round the World" is associated with which player?
A. Gar Heard
B. Michael Jordan
C. Ray Allen

199. DeMarcus Cousins joined which team in the 2018-19 season?
A. Golden State Warriors
B. Los Angeles Lakers
C. Houston Rockets

200. Who holds the record for the fastest triple-double in NBA history?
A. Russell Westbrook
B. Nikola Jokic
C. Magic Johnson

201. The 1988 NBA Eastern Conference champions were?
A. Chicago Bulls
B. Detroit Pistons
C. Boston Celtics

202. Toronto Raptors' first pick in the 2009 NBA draft was?
A. Demar DeRozan

B. Terrence Ross

C. Jonas Valanciunas

203. Los Angeles Lakers, and which other team, played in the 2009
Finals?

A. Boston Celtics

B. Orlando Magic

C. San Antonio Spurs

204. Who shoots the most 3s in the NBA?

A. James Harden

B. Stephen Curry

C. Klay Thompson

205. Miami Heat was represented by which player in the 2018 All-Stars
game?

A. Bam Adebayo

B. Goran Dragic

C. Jimmy Butler

206. Which team finished first in the Southeast Division for the 2017-18
season?

A. Orlando Magic

B. Miami Heat

C. Charlotte Hornets

207. Tristan Thompson's first NBA start was as a replacement: True or
False?

A. False

B. True

208. The highest-paid player in NBA history is?

A. LeBron James

B. Stephen Curry

C. Kevin Durant

209. Which player was replaced for Tristan Thompson's first NBA start?
A. Anderson Varejao
B. Al Horford
C. Joakim Noah

210. Who has the most dunks (3) in a single jump?
A. Dwight Howard
B. JaVale McGee
C. Nate Robinson

211. Who won the 2011 NBA Slam Dunk Contest?
A. Blake Griffin
B. Serge Ibaka
C. JaVale McGee

212. The 2008 Finals MVP was?
A. Paul Pierce
B. Kobe Bryant
C. Kevin Garnett

213. What object did Blake Griffin dunk over in the 2011 Slam Dunk Contest?
A. A bench
B. The hood of a car
C. A mascot

214. Who won the Defensive Player of the Year in 2016?
A. Draymond Green
B. Kawhi Leonard
C. Rudy Gobert

215. How many points do you get for a basket made from the free-throw line?

A. 2 points

B. 1 point

C. 3 points

216. The NBA Rookie of the Year for the 2010-11 season was?

A. Blake Griffin

B. John Wall

C. DeMarcus Cousins

217. A regular NBA season game lasts for how long?

A. 48 minutes

B. 40 minutes

C. 60 minutes

218. Jeremy Lin played for which team in 2012?

A. Golden State Warriors

B. New York Knicks

C. Houston Rockets

219. Which Italian player was selected in the first round of the 2008 NBA Draft?

A. Andrea Bargnani

B. Danilo Gallinari

C. Marco Belinelli

220. Ricky Rubio's NBA debut was in which year?

A. 2009

B. 2011

C. 2012

221. The first player to average a triple-double for a season was?

A. Russell Westbrook

B. Oscar Robertson

C. Magic Johnson

222. Who won the MVP in the 2018 All-Star Game?

A. Stephen Curry

B. LeBron James

C. Kevin Durant

223. Which player holds the record for the most All-Star games played with 14?

A. Tim Duncan

B. Kobe Bryant

C. Kareem Abdul-Jabbar

224. John Wall missed the 2018 NBA Finals due to?

A. Shoulder injury

B. Knee injury

C. Personal reasons

225. The record for most assists in a single NBA Finals game (21) is held by?

A. Magic Johnson

B. John Stockton

C. Jason Kidd

226. Zion Williamson holds a degree in?

A. Business management

B. Creative writing

C. Sports psychology

227. The 13th overall pick in the 1996 NBA Draft was?

A. Steve Nash

B. Kobe Bryant

C. Derek Fisher

228. Which player was nicknamed "Iceman"?

A. George Gervin

B. Julius Erving

C. Michael Jordan

229. Which player has played the most games in Golden State Warriors history?

A. Klay Thompson

B. Stephen Curry

C. Chris Mullin

230. Who won Coach of the Year for the 1985-86 season?

A. Pat Riley

B. Mike Fratello

C. Chuck Daly

231. The Detroit Pistons were initially called?

A. Fort Wayne Pistons

B. Fort Wayne Zollner Pistons

C. Flint Tropics

232. The postseason record for most steals in a single game is held by?

A. Allen Iverson

B. Chris Paul

C. John Stockton

233. LeBron James was told to "shut up and dribble" by?

A. A Fox employee

B. A news anchor

C. A politician

234. The NBA Coach of the Year in 1993 was?
A. Pat Riley
B. Phil Jackson
C. Larry Brown

235. How many NBA Finals did Wilt Chamberlain play in during his career?
A. 6
B. 5
C. 7

236. The youngest player to reach 10,000 points in 2003 was?
A. LeBron James
B. Kobe Bryant
C. Kevin Garnett

237. Jonas Jerebko is from which country?
A. Sweden
B. Denmark
C. Finland

238. Derrick Williams started how many games in his rookie season?
A. 12 games
B. 15 games
C. 20 games

239. Which team did Magic Johnson play for in 1980?
A. Boston Celtics
B. Los Angeles Lakers
C. Philadelphia 76ers

240. The first NBA All-Star Game was held where?

A. New York

B. Boston Garden

C. Chicago Stadium

241. Tyronn Lue was the assistant coach for which team in 2012?

A. Cleveland Cavaliers

B. Celtics

C. Golden State Warriors

242. The head coach of Team Steph in the 2018 All-Star Game was?

A. Steve Kerr

B. Mike D'Antoni

C. Gregg Popovich

243. Who is Hugo the Hornet?

A. The mascot of the Charlotte Hornets

B. A former player

C. A fan nickname

244. Who was nicknamed "Air Ball"?

A. Michael Jordan

B. Scottie Pippen

C. Kobe Bryant

245. Overtime is played if there is a tie at the end of what?

A. Fourth quarter

B. A regulation period

C. Third quarter

246. What is DeMarcus Cousins' nickname?

A. The Big Diesel

B. Boogie

C. The Brow

247. Which team did Nikola Vucevic play for in his rookie season?
A. Orlando Magic
B. Philadelphia 76ers
C. Los Angeles Lakers

248. Which city named its team the Grizzlies?
A. Memphis
B. Vancouver
C. Seattle

249. Marc Gasol delayed his NBA rookie season to play a year in which country?
A. Spain
B. Italy
C. France

250. Which city in Britain is home to the Giants?
A. London
B. Manchester
C. Birmingham

Open Ended Questions

251. The Rocks are from which city?

252. Which city in Britain are the Eagles from?

253. The force is from which city in Britain?

254. The team that waived Luol Deng in 2018 was?

255. Which person can call a timeout in the NBA?

256. How many NBA arenas are there in the United States?

257. When a player fails to dribble while moving, what happens?

258. The standard dimension for an NBA basketball court is?

259. The hoop has three basic parts; the rim, net, and?

260. Which team drafted Ray Allen?

261. Which NBA player was nicknamed Pink Panther?

262. Wilt Chamberlain set an all-time single-game rebound record in a single game against the Boston Celtics in 1960. How many rebounds was it?

263. What is the name of Shaquille O'Neal's first single that was released in 1993?

264. Who won the MVP in the first all-star game?

265. Which player has the same name as the Twitter logo?

266. Chris Webber was initially drafted by which club?

267. Which number did Kobe Bryant have in the 1996 draft?

268. Orlando Magic drafted Chris Webber but traded him for who?

269. When a ball handler throws the ball near the basket to their teammates to dunk it, what is it called?

270. How many NBA Championships did Sam Jones win with the Boston Celtics?

271. What happens when a player commits an FFP2?

272. The different ways that possession of the ball goes from one team to another are called?

273. A fast-paced offensive play style in basketball is called?

274. How many NBA Finals did Shawn Kemp play in his career?

275. Who is sometimes referred to as "The Human Victory Cigar"?

276. What does BEEF mean in basketball?

277. The legal way to make a steal in basketball is by?

278. What type of foul is kicking a basketball in a game?

279. How many playoff appearances has Anthony Edwards made from 2021 to 2024?

280. What was the first coin-op arcade machine to be Sports-licensed?

281. The first basketball used what as goals?

282. Traveling results in infractions, True or False?

283. A defensive player can stand in the paint without guarding anyone for how long?

284. Which college did Sydney Wicks attend?

285. The tallest player in the 1992 Dream team was?

286. How Much fine did Michael Jordan pay each time he wore the Air Jordan?

287. Who is the Golden State Warrior's all-time leading scorer?

288. The team that had the shortest and tallest players in NBA history at the same time was?

289. What is the name of the first team based outside the United States to win an NBA title?

290. Who performed the grandfather's role in the Pacific Northwest Ballet performance of The Nutcracker?

291. Which Disney character did Tim Duncan tattoo to his skin?

292. How many NBA Finals did James Worthy play in his career?

293. Who was the first player drafted out of high school?

294. Rapper Drake is a fan of which NBA team?

295. The main inspiration for the NBA jam was?

296. Which year did the Antonio Spurs sweep the Cleveland Cavaliers 4-0 in a final?

297. The nickname of Cedric Maxwell was?

298. Which club is Cedric Maxwell known to be a legend?

299. Which player has played the most number of games in Chicago Bulls history as of 2024?

300. Which NBA player was called "Fall Back Baby" by announcer Chick Hearn?

301. How many NBA titles did Dick Barnett win in his career?

302. Who has the most blocks in Los Angeles Lakers history?

303. Dirk Nowitzki was from which country?

304. What is it called when a basketball player falls too easily on the floor to try and get a foul?

305. How many NBA playoffs did Nenad Krstic reach in his career?

306. The NBA team from Indiana is called?

307. The Toronto NBA basketball team is called?

308. The nickname of the duke basketball team is?

309. The style of play that focuses on running and has no center is called?

310. Jonas Jerebko is from which country?

311. When a player scores a point, what is it called?

312. The NBA team from Oklahoma is called?

313. The NBA team from Brooklyn is called?

314. Who has the most assists in Boston Celtics history?

315. When a player legally deflects a shot, what is it called?

316. The NBA team from Phoenix is called?

317. How many seasons did Mirza Teletovic play in the NBA?

318. Marco Belinelli is from which country?

319. Ray Allen's first name is?

320. The NBA team from Detroit is known as the?

321. James Harden's primary position is?

322. The arena for both LA-based teams is called?

323. Karl Malone, known as "The Mailman," spent most of his career playing for which team?

324. Moses Malone was the first player in modern basketball to go directly to the NBA from which setting?

325. Stephen Curry wore which jersey number for the Golden State Warriors?

326. Which color does the majority of NBA teams wear at home?

327. What is Pete Maravich nickname?

328. The first name of Magic Johnson is?

329. The NBA team from Dallas is called?

330. The NBA team from Milwaukee is called?

331. Who has the most blocks in Miami Heat history?

332. The team from Minnesota is called?

333. The NBA team from Utah is known as the?

334. Who were the Twin Towers that played for Houston?

335. The team from New Orleans is called?

336. The NBA team from San Antonio is called?

337. When Carmelo Anthony was with the New York Knicks, what jersey number did he wear?

338. Who leads the NBA in missed shots as of 2024?

339. The NBA team from Miami is called?

340. The N in the NBA is called?

341. The area where basketball is played is called?

342. The basketball team from Sacramento is called?

343. Jonas Valanciunas is from which country?

344. Who is the youngest player in NBA history to record at least 13,000 points?

345. Dirk Nowitzki's number for the Dallas Mavericks is?

346. The name of the Chicago-based team is?

347. Who logged the NBA's first triple-double on December 14, 1950?

348. Kevin McHale spent his entire career with which team?

349. What NBA team was the first to win 70 games in one season?

350. George Mikan was so dominant that his play led to the introduction of which NBA rule?

351. The Hall of Fame for the NBA is called?

352. How many NBA titles did CJ Watson win in his career?

353. Russell Westbrook wore which number for the US in the 2012 Olympics?

354. Kentavious Pope came in which number pick in the 2013 NBA draft?

355. John Jenkins came in which number pick in the 2012 NBA draft?

356. Dennis Schroder came in which number pick in the 2013 NBA draft?

357. Meyers Leonard came in which number pick in the 2012 NBA draft?

358. The inventor of basketball is from which country?

359. How many All-Star games did DeMar DeRozan make?

360. The lines at either end of the basketball court are called?

361. In the opening game of the 2012-13 season, what was the score between the Heat and Celtics?

362. Gorgui Dieng was picked by which team in the 2013 NBA draft?

363. What was the score in the 2000 all-star game?

364. How many NBA titles did Michael Kid-Gilchrist win in his career?

365. Hakeem Olajuwon, known for his "Dream Shake" move, won back-to-back championships with which NBA team?

366. Miami Heat played in the 2021 NBA finals. Yes or No?

367. Robert Parish, known as "The Chief," won most of his championships with which NBA team?

368. The Phoenix Suns were knocked out of the 2006 NBA playoffs by which team?

369. How NBA teams drafted Chandler Parson in 2011?

370. Which NBA team drafted James Young in 2014?

371. The basketball video game that featured superhuman dunks was?

372. Bob Pettit was the first player in NBA history to win what award twice?

373. How many NBA titles did Adreian Payne win in his career?

374. Which team selected Cody Zeller as a 4th pick in the 2013 NBA draft?

375. What was David Robinson's nickname?

376. Dolph Schayes played most of his career with which NBA team?

377. Did Udonis Haslem play for the Miami Heat? Yes or No?

378. Which team drafted Taj Gibson in 2009?

379. What was Allen Iverson's nickname in the 2005-6 season?

380. Which team selected Julius Randle as the seventh overall pick in the 2014 NBA draft?

381. How many NBA championships has Kevin Durant won in 2024?

382. Kobe Bryant wore which number in the 2012 Olympics?

383. How many NBA titles did CJ Wilcox win in his career?

384. Ray McCallum came in which number pick in the 2013 NBA draft?

385. For much of his time with the Chicago Bulls, which shirt number did Michael Jordan wear?

386. Isiah Thomas was known for leading which team to two consecutive NBA championships in the late 1980s?

387. Which NBA team selected Jerami Grant in the 39th overall pick in the 2014 NBA draft?

388. Maurice Harkless came in which number pick in the 2012 NBA draft?

389. Which organization certified Michael Jordan, as a billionaire?

390. Which NBA team drafted Chase Budinger in 2009?

391. PJ Hairston came in which number pick in the 2014 NBA draft?

392. Nate Thurmond was the first player in NBA history to record a quadruple-double while playing for which team?

393. Which NBA team was the first to hire a woman on their coaching staff?

394. In 2004 an altercation occurred mid-game between two teams in an incident that became known as 'Malice at the Palace'. Which two teams were involved?

395. Anthony Bennett came in which number pick in the 2013 NBA draft?

396. Nemanja Nedovic came in which number pick in the 2013 NBA draft?

397. Which NBA team drafted Glen Rice Jnr in the 2013 NBA draft?

398. How many NBA championships did Bill Walton win?

399. In Miami Heat, what number does Chris Bosh wear?

400. Who has the most blocks in Chicago Bulls history?

401. Which NBA team plays at the Target Center?

402. Which NBA team drafted Alex Len in the 2013 NBA draft?

403. Who was the No. 1 pick in the 2024 NBA Draft?

404. Which team was Kobe Bryant playing for in 2000?

405. The NBA logo is said to be inspired by which legendary player?

406. Golden State Warriors were originally from what city?

407. Which NBA team plays at the American Airlines Center?

408. In the 2012 NBA draft, what was Anthony Davis's number pick?

409. How many times was Kevin Love an all-star?

410. The Rockets basketball team is based in?

411. The Heat is based in which place?

412. How many rings does James Harden have?

413. Which NBA team plays at the Ball Arena?

414. Lenny Wilkens is unique for being inducted into the Hall of Fame as both a player and what?

415. TN Bobcats are based in which place?

416. John Wooden went to which high school?

417. Demar DeRozan played for which team during the 2014 playoffs?

418. The most valuable player in the NBA finals 2005-6 was?

419. The uncontested shot is when a basketball shot can be attempted without defensive interference. True or False?

420. In the 2014 playoffs, which team did Patty Mills play for?

421. What is James Worthy's popular nickname?

422. In the 2012-13 Pacific division, the LA Clippers finished in which position?

423. How many championships does McGee have?

424. How many rebounds did Udonis Haslem make in the 2011 NBA finals?

425. How many NBA Championships did Nate Archibald win in his career?

426. Did Stephen Curry share the points total in the 2013 playoffs? Yes or No?

427. Which team was O'Neal playing for in 2000?

428. Which French player appeared in the 2009 NBA game live?

429. Derrick Rose played college basketball where?

430. Which team won the Atlantic division in the 2012-13 season?

431. Magic Johnson played college basketball where?

432. What must a player do when in possession of the ball?

433. Detroit Pistons play their home matches where?

434. Which arena do the Suns play their home in?

435. Kobe Bryant entered the NBA straight from high school. True or False?

436. The Golden State Warriors participated in the 2014 first-round match. Yes or No?

437. Which high school did Kobe Bryant go to?

438. The Golden State Warriors player who scored 13 rebounds in the final game of their 2014 foray round match was?

439. How many NBA teams did Danny Green play for in his career?

440. Draymond Green played for which team in 2013?

441. The Detroit Pistons were originally called what?

442. Who has the nickname black mamba?

443. The duo that was the highlight of the Laker's win in the NBA 2000-2002 championship was?

444. Which NBA team plays its home game at the Barclays Center?

445. Which city do the Grizzlies play their home match?

446. What team ended the Phoenix Suns' run and knocked them out of the 2006 NBA Playoffs?

447. Luka Doncic played professionally for which European team before joining the NBA?

448. What is Giannis Antetokounmpo nickname?

449. How many NBA Championship titles did Paul Arizin win in his career?

450. How many NBA Finals did Charles Barkley play in his career?

451. The person with the most 40-point game in NBA history was?

452. How many games did LeBron James play before reaching 20000 points?

453. The person with more rings than Jordan is?

454. Has LeBron James won an Oscar in the past? Yes or No?

455. How many rings does Bill Russell have?

456. When the ball is dead, a timeout is requested. True or False?

457. All substitutions are legal for both teams during a timeout. True or False?

458. After a time has been out in a basketball game, what happens to the clocks?

459. A timeout can be granted only at what time?

460. When a timeout is called because a player is injured, the play can resume even when the injured player is still on the pitch. Yes or No?

461. A timeout shall not be granted to the defensive team during what?

462. A successful free throw attempt counts as how many points?

463. If there is a discrepancy in the score and it cannot be resolved, what happens?

464. It is a violation for a player to attempt a field goal at an opponent's basket. True or False?

465. A discrepancy in the score can be resolved. True or False?

466. A field goal accidentally scored in the opponent's basket shall be added to?

467. An unsuccessful free throw attempt that is tapped into the basket counts as how many points?

468. A successful field goal from inside the three-point area is counted as how many points.

469. A successful field goal from outside the three-point area is counted as how many points?

470. Officials can permit players with jewelry to play in a basketball game. Yes, or No?

471. Players are allowed to use foreign substances during and before the game. Yes, or No?

472. The recommended ball pressure should be between 7 ½ pounds and?

473. What is the name of the official who is in charge of the game?

474. Who makes the final rulings on all replays?

475. Which official checks the active list of players before the game?

476. The youngest player to reach 30000 points was?

477. Shai Gilgeous-Alexander was originally drafted by which NBA team?

478. Jayson Tatum set a franchise record for most points in a single playoff game with which NBA team?

479. The most missed shots in the NBA go to which player?

480. How many NBA players have had 60 or more points in more than one game?

481. The person who had the shortest NBA career was?

482. Which NBA team plays its home game at the Capital One Arena?

483. The mamba, Kobe Bryant's nickname, often refers to which animal?

484. The best NBA record was?

485. Has Stephen Curry ever missed a free throw? Yes or No.

486. What was Jason Kapono's best three-point shot percentage?

487. What was Steve Novak's best three-point shot percentage?

488. What was Stephen Curry's best three-point shot percentage?

489. Who was the youngest player ever to play in the NBA?

490. How many seconds did James Curry spend in his NBA career?

491. The oldest rookie in the NBA was?

492. The first NBA team was?

493. Which NBA team plays its home game at the Chase Center?

494. How old was Prigioni when he became an NBA rookie?

495. How tall is Boban Marjanovic?

496. How tall is Kristaps Porzingis?

497. The youngest Lakers player is?

498. The heaviest NBA player was?

499. Which player had the most ejections in the NBA?

500. The lowest-scoring NBA game was between the Fort Wayne Pistons and?

501. Whose record did LeBron James break as the All-time leading playoff scorer?

502. How old was Derrick Rose when he won the MVP?

503. Michael Jordan retired at what age?

504. When was the New York Knicks formed?

505. Who is the shortest NBA player to slam dunk?

506. Who founded the New York Knicks?

507. Scott Perry has coached the New York Knicks. Yes or No?

508. Gary Payton played for the Thunder. Yes or No?

509. The first person who dunked in the NBA was?

510. Kobe Bryant's vertical is?

511. The highest vertical in the NBA was done by who?

512. Which NBA player missed a record number of 23 free throws in 2016 against the Rockets?

513. In 1990, which Orlando Magic player had 30 assists in a game?

514. The most personal foul in NBA history is held by who?

515. Cal Bowdler once had 10 personal fouls in a game, True or False?

516. In 1997, Bubba Wells was disqualified for fouls. True or False?

517. Which year did the Phoenix Suns score 107 points in a half?

518. Which NBA team had a 33-game winning streak in the 1971-72 season?

519. Dwight Howard played in the 2012 season? Yes or No?

520. The highest assist James Harden had in a season was?

521. From 1976 to 1995, how many career rebounds did Malone make?

522. Wilt Chamberlain's number was retired by?

523. Which other sport did Dave Debusschre also play professionally?

524. Chris Webber played one game for the team that drafted him. True or False?

525. Which NBA team plays its home game at the Delta Center?

526. Muggsy Bogues was a second-round pick. True or False?

527. What is the name of the first basketball team Toronto had?

528. After Paul Pierce was stabbed 11 times, he still played every game in the 2000-1 season? Yes or No?

529. Which hand does LeBron James write with?

530. Which player has played the most number of games in Boston Celtics history?

531. In 1991, which team made a 68-point margin in victory?

532. Which year did the Utah Jazz have a 36-point comeback?

533. In the 3-point Era, who had 23,334 career points without a made 3-pointer?

534. Calvin Murphy's free throw percentage of 95.81 records stood for how many years?

535. Who has the most assists in Chicago Bulls history?

536. Which did Joel Anthony have 29 minutes in a game without rebounds, steals, assists, or blocks?

537. From 1976 to 1995, Moses Malone made how many career offensive rebounds?

538. Which Utah Jazz player has the record for the most number of assists?

539. How many seconds is each team entitled to replace a disqualified player?

540. All periods of regulation play in the NBA are how many minutes?

541. All overtime plays are how many minutes?

542. How many minutes is given to each of the halves?

543. The game is considered to be _____ minutes parts when the clock shows 2:00 or less.

544. In each period, who is supposed to announce that two minutes are remaining?

545. Each period ends when what happens?

546. When the official blows his whistle, what happens to the timing devices?

547. The official can use the official time to allow a player to change or repair equipment. Yes or No?

548. Each team is entitled to how many timeouts?

549. In the fourth period, how many timeouts are each team limited to?

550. In overtime periods, how many timeouts does a team have?

Interesting Basketball Facts

1. The first official game of basketball was played in Springfield, Massachusetts, using two peach baskets as goals and a soccer ball in place of a basketball.

2. Dribbling wasn't allowed when basketball first started. Instead, each player had to pass from where they caught the ball, until Yale's team introduced dribbling in 1897, forever changing the game.

3. The first basketball game had 18 players on the court—nine per side—matching the number of people who turned up to play on that historic day.

4. Believe it or not, shouldering, pushing, or tripping an opponent wasn't a foul until 1910, when official rules finally introduced these penalties.

5. In 1969, the San Francisco Warriors made a surprisingly picked a high school girl named Denise Long, who averaged an incredible 68.2 points per game. She remains one of the NBA's most unique draft selections.

6. Darryl Dawkins' powerful dunks shattered so many backboards that the NBA eventually introduced breakaway rims to keep the game going without broken glass.

7. Willis Reed stands out as the only second-round NBA draft pick to go on to win an MVP award, an exceptional rarity in league history.

8. Michael Jordan, "The GOAT," has a record-high playoff scoring average with 33.4 points per game—a feat no other player has surpassed in postseason play.

9. LeBron James has played the most playoff games and scored the most total points in NBA playoff history, proving his longevity and consistency.

10. Wilt Chamberlain holds the all-time NBA record for the most rebounds—a legacy of his physicality and unmatched presence on the court.

11. Kobe Bryant is the only player to post 600+ points, 100+ rebounds, and 100+ assists across three straight playoff seasons, a testament to his all-around dominance.

12. Magic Johnson and John Stockton share the record for the most assists in a single playoff game, displaying their legendary passing skills.

13. Shaquille O'Neal owns the playoff record for most offensive rebounds, showcasing his power and tenacity under the rim.

14. Allen Iverson holds the record for most steals in a single NBA playoff game, a highlight of his quickness and intensity on defense.

15. Kareem Abdul-Jabbar won six regular-season MVP awards, more than any other player, solidifying his place in basketball history.

16. Rasheed Wallace set an NBA single-season record with 41 technical fouls in 2000-2001, showing just how fiery his passion for the game was.

17. Bubba Wells holds the record for the fastest foul-out, exiting an NBA game in just 2 minutes and 43 seconds.

18. Just a year after basketball was invented, women played their first official game in 1892—a swift adoption that added momentum to the sport's growth.

19. The NBA's iconic logo silhouette is modeled after Lakers legend Jerry West, capturing his classic shooting form.

20. The first NBA game took place on November 1, 1946, with the New York Knicks edging out the Toronto Huskies in a close 68-66 win.

21. Led by Wilt Chamberlain, the 1971-72 Lakers hold the record for the longest NBA winning streak, with 33 consecutive victories.

22. The NBA's salary cap is designed to level the playing field, setting a limit on how much teams can spend on player salaries to avoid wealthy teams "buying" championships.

23. At 5'3", Muggsy Bogues remains the smallest player in NBA history, proving that size doesn't define a player's success.

24. Chris Webber was drafted first by the Orlando Magic in 1993, but he never played for them—they immediately traded him to the Golden State Warriors for Penny Hardaway.

25. Known as a multi-talented athlete, Dave DeBusschere not only excelled as a forward but also spent two seasons in Major League Baseball.

26. Ray Allen's real name is actually Walter, a little-known fact about one of the best three-point shooters in NBA history.

27. Did you know Pau Gasol attended medical school? The Spanish forward considered a career in medicine before dedicating himself to basketball.

28. Rasheed Wallace, known for his unique flair, had his NBA championship ring custom-made to fit his middle finger.

29. Wilt Chamberlain had his jersey number retired by the Harlem Globetrotters—a rare honor for a player who famously scored 100 points in a single NBA game.

30. The three-point shot wasn't always a part of basketball; it originated in the ABA and only made its way to the NBA in the 1979-80 season.

31. Carmelo Anthony once introduced himself as "Tyrone" in school because he thought classmates and teachers couldn't pronounce his real name.

32. Before his NBA career, Vince Carter served as a drum major in high school, demonstrating his early love for rhythm and teamwork.

33. Standing 7'7", Manute Bol once recounted how he killed a lion with a spear—a story that captures the former player's legendary bravery.

34. In the early days, a jump ball followed every basket, making for a more physically demanding game.

35. The Raptors originally drafted Antawn Jamison in 1998 but immediately traded him to Golden State in exchange for Vince Carter.

36. Surprisingly, Kobe Bryant wasn't a top-10 draft pick; he was selected 13th overall by the Charlotte Hornets before being traded to the Lakers.

37. During Bill Russell's career, the Celtics reached the NBA Finals numerous times, losing only once, making his era one of near-total dominance.

38. Elvin Hayes, despite his immense talent and achievements, never won an MVP award—a surprising omission in NBA history.

39. NBA champion and Hall of Famer Bill Bradley also served as a three-term U.S. senator and presidential candidate, highlighting his diverse career.

40. Wilt Chamberlain, as a rookie, led the league in scoring with an incredible 37.6 points per game, setting a high bar right from the start.

41. The largest margin of victory in an NBA game occurred when the Cleveland Cavaliers defeated the Miami Heat by a staggering 148-80.

42. Coaching legend Larry Brown has the unique distinction of coaching both college and professional basketball, bringing his expertise to multiple levels of the sport.

43. In a memorable playoff moment, Isiah Thomas scored 16 points in just 94 seconds, though his Pistons still lost the game.

44. While Wilt Chamberlain scored countless points, George Yardley was the first to hit 2,000 in a single season, doing so in 1957-58 for the Detroit Pistons.

45. Allen Iverson, known for his tenacity, holds the record for the most steals in an NBA playoff game, a testament to his defensive prowess.

46. The Miami Heat remains the only NBA team to have won both the Slam Dunk Contest and Three-Point Shootout in the same All-Star weekend.

47. Dikembe Mutombo, famous for his shot-blocking, made the All-Star team as a rookie for the Denver Nuggets, though he lost Rookie of the Year to Larry Johnson.

48. The 1996-97 Phoenix Suns went from a 13-game losing streak to a 10-game winning streak in one season, showing resilience in an up-and-down year.

49. Shawn Kemp's middle initial "T" doesn't stand for anything—he added it as a stylistic choice.

50. Despite his iconic career, Charles Barkley only played organized basketball for two years in high school.

51. The Celtics and the Knicks are the only NBA teams to have never relocated since their founding.

52. Michael Jordan, surprisingly, was not the first pick in the 1984 NBA Draft; Hakeem Olajuwon was chosen before him.

53. The first slam dunk in recorded history happened in 1936, performed by a Texan named Joe Fortenberry, though it was likened to "dipping a roll in coffee" back then.

54. The NBA's first Black coach was Boston Celtics star Bill Russell, hired in 1966 to lead the team as a player-coach.

55. The three-point line wasn't introduced until 1979 after years of debate on its impact on the game.

56. Studies show that 60% of NBA players go broke within five years of retirement, despite lucrative salaries during their careers.

57. Only two NBA games have ever been played on Christmas Eve.

58. The old Twitter logo was named after Boston Celtics legend Larry Bird, paying homage to his greatness.

59. Let me know if you'd like more examples from the list!

60. When Michael Jordan debuted the first Air Jordans, the NBA banned them due to their color, and he was fined every game he wore them.

61. One in every six American men over 7 feet tall has played in the NBA, an impressive rate showing the unique appeal of height in basketball.

62. Although 5-foot-3 Muggsy Bogues and 7-foot-7 Manute Bol were teammates, Bogues once claimed he blocked Bol's shot in a one-on-one game, although it wasn't an official NBA event.

63. When James Naismith first invented basketball, the game consisted of two 15-minute halves with a 5-minute break in between.

64. Basketball entered the Olympic Games in 1936, further solidifying its place on the global sports stage.

65. The NBA, originally known as the Basketball Association of America, was officially established in 1946, marking the beginning of professional basketball as we know it.

66. Canada was the first country outside the U.S. to adopt basketball, spreading the sport internationally from its birthplace.

67. Basketball quickly went global, with France playing in 1893, England in 1894, and Australia, India, China, and Japan joining in by 1900.

68. Early basketball uniforms were vastly different, featuring knee-length football trousers, jersey tights, padded shorts, and knee guards.

69. Wilt Chamberlain's 100-point game against the New York Knicks in 1962 is still the highest point total by any player in an NBA game.

70. "Jumping Joe" Fulks set a postseason record for the most missed field goals in a game, missing 38 against the St. Louis Bombers.

71. When Michael Jordan first wore Air Jordans, the NBA fined him $5,000 per game because they violated the league's uniform color policy.

72. The longest NBA game lasted an astounding 6 overtimes, with the Indianapolis Olympians eventually beating the Rochester Royals in 1951.

73. Unlike most NBA courts, the Boston Celtics' court is made from red oak hardwood, adding a distinctive touch to their home arena.

74. Many NBA players have unique free-throw routines. Karl Malone famously whispered a silent prayer before each shot.

75. Pablo Prigioni was the oldest rookie in NBA history, making his debut with the New York Knicks at age 35 in 2012.

76. Earl Lloyd was the first African American player in an NBA game, debuting for the Washington Capitols in 1950.

77. LeBron James' chalk toss ritual—throwing chalk dust into the air before games—has become an iconic pre-game tradition.

78. March Madness, the NCAA's annual tournament, has become a global event with millions of fans following the collegiate competition every spring.

79. Occasionally, NBA coaches will throw a towel onto the court to express disagreement with a call or to pump up their team.

80. The Atlanta Hawks made a quirky draft pick in 1974 when GM Pat Williams "selected" his newborn son, who had just been born on draft day.

81. In 1984, the Chicago Bulls drafted Carl Lewis, who went on to win four gold medals in the Los Angeles Olympics, despite having no basketball experience.

82. Even superstars Wilt Chamberlain and Oscar Robertson weren't selected No. 1 in the NBA Draft, despite their legendary potential.

83. In a humorous twist, the Philadelphia 76ers drafted the owner's friend in the 1983 draft, picking Norman Horvitz from the Philadelphia School of Pharmacy.

84. Seven NBA teams have never held the first overall draft pick: Denver, Indiana, Memphis, Miami, Oklahoma City, Phoenix, and Utah.

85. Duke and Kentucky hold the record for the most No. 1 NBA draft picks, each producing three top selections.

86. The first non-college player to go No. 1 was Kwame Brown in the 2001 NBA Draft, opening the door for other high school stars.

87. Dennis Rodman, known for his rebounding, is the only second-rounder from the Magic/Bird era to be inducted into the Hall of Fame.

88. In every NBA draft between 2002 and 2013, at least one player selected was the son of a former NBA player, showing a legacy of talent in the league.

89. The 1968 NBA draft stretched 21 rounds, with teams picking until the Bulls used the final pick at No. 214, making it one of the longest drafts in history.

90. Ten players from the NBA's 50 Greatest Players list were selected as No. 1 picks, including stars like Magic Johnson and Shaquille O'Neal.

91. Chicago Bulls fans were shocked when team owner Donald Sterling offered five players and two first-round picks to trade for Michael Jordan, an offer that was rejected.

92. The San Antonio Spurs have only been in the draft lottery three times in their history, a testament to their consistent success.

93. Until 1985, the No. 1 NBA draft pick was decided by a coin toss between the worst teams in each conference, before the lottery system was implemented.

94. Yao Ming became the first international player without college experience to be chosen first overall, marking a milestone in 2002.

95. The 2003 NBA draft, featuring LeBron James, Dwyane Wade, Carmelo Anthony, and Chris Bosh, is considered one of the best drafts in recent history.

96. The NBA began televising its draft in 1980, the same year other leagues like the NFL and NHL did the same.

97. Since the lottery began, the Cleveland Cavaliers have landed the No. 1 pick more times than any other team.

98. Only four of the 39 players drafted first overall through the 2022-23 season won championships with their original team.

99. The Golden State Warriors set an NBA record with a 73-9 regular season in 2016, the best in league history.

100. The Los Angeles Lakers hold the record for the longest winning streak in a season, with 33 consecutive wins.

101. With only seven wins in the 2011-12 season, the Charlotte Bobcats set the record for the worst season in NBA history.

102. With over 38,652 career points, LeBron James currently stands as the NBA's all-time scoring leader, solidifying his legacy as one of the game's greats.

Answers to Trivia Questions

1. 1946
2. Derrick Rose
3. sky hook
4. Domantas Sabonis
5. Wilt Chamberlain
6. 2020-21
7. 11
8. Cleveland Cavs
9. Denver Nuggets
10. The Basketball Association of America
11. Julius Erving
12. 1984
13. Chicago Bulls
14. Shaquille O'Neal
15. Running jump shot
16. The Round Mound of Rebound
17. 5 players
18. Ron Artest
19. 21
20. Yes
21. 1951
22. Thunderstruck
23. Earl Lloyd
24. Wilt Chamberlain
25. 5 in 40-minute game or 6 in a 48-minute game
26. 10
27. Underhand free throw
28. 10 seconds
29. Goaltending

30. Anthony Davis
31. Tom Heinsohn
32. Personal foul
33. Klay Thompson
34. Charlotte Hornets
35. Traveling
36. 13
37. Atlanta Hawks
38. Charles Barkley
39. Three parts
40. Unlimited.
41. Jalen Rose
42. 24 cm
43. Minnesota Timberwolves
44. Canada
45. James Harden
46. Houston Rockets
47. Jump ball
48. The Dream
49. 12 minutes
50. Orlando Magic
51. Dribbling violation
52. Anthony 'Spud' Webb (5'7")
53. Power forward
54. Jeffrey
55. Los Angeles Lakers
56. James Naismith
57. The Boston Celtics
58. NBA
59. Atlanta Hawks
60. Power Forward
61. 1946

62. Ed Sadowski

63. Sam Cassell

64. Dallas Maverick

65. 30 teams

66. Kangaroo Kid

67. Indiana Pacers

68. Thunder Dan

69. Chicago White Sox

70. Golden State Warriors

71. 3 points

72. Portland Trailblazers

73. True

74. Boston Celtics

75. 1995

76. 1979

77. Karl Malone

78. The Phoenix Suns

79. 2013

80. Point guard

81. The Los Angeles Lakers

82. David Robinson

83. DeAndre Ayton

84. 100 seconds

85. Karl Malone

86. Kobe Bryant

87. Dwayne Wade

88. 3 referees

89. Bill Russell

90. True

91. Danny Biasone

92. 1

93. True

94. 1948

95. Zach LaVine

96. Marc Gasol

97. Nate Robinson

98. 5 titles

99. King James

100. USA Basketball (The USAB)

101. 7

102. Charles Barkley

103. Boston Celtics

104. 1971

105. Harold Hunter

106. Philadelphia 76ers

107. Denver Nuggets

108. A Japanese American, Wataru Misaka

109. South Africa

110. Lamar Odom

111. Kareem Abdul

112. Lob city

113. Kareem Abdul

114. Los Angeles Lakers

115. Lithuania

116. Kobe Bryant

117. Wes Unseld

118. Detroit Falcons

119. True

120. 9

121. Sky

122. The Suns

123. 2006

124. True

125. Medical school

126. Chris s Singleton
127. Derrick Rose
128. Washington Capitols
129. the Los Angeles Lakers
130. Springfield Massachusetts
131. 69
132. Foot locker
133. San Francisco
134. New Jersey Jets
135. Michael Jordan
136. Victor Oladipo
137. George Yardley
138. 1985
139. Walt Frazier
140. Maple planks
141. Spencer Dinwiddie
142. Scott Skiles
143. Darko Milicic
144. True
145. Brooklyn
146. Nat Hickey
147. 2015
148. Tyrone Bogues
149. Miami Heat
150. The Knicks
151. 22
152. 1611
153. New York Knicks
154. Derrick Rose
155. Clyde
156. Serge Ibaka
157. Two times

158. John Stockton
159. Carmelo Anthony
160. Olivier Rioux
161. Dwight Howard
162. 4 games
163. John Stockton
164. Philadelphia Warriors
165. 1984.
166. Donovan Mitchell
167. Darryl Dawkins
168. Ed Macauley
169. Brooklyn
170. Alvin Robertson
171. Willis Reed
172. Hakeem Olajuwon
173. 1970
174. Russell Westbrook
175. China
176. Charlotte Bobcats
177. 2015 finals
178. Cleveland Cavaliers
179. 2011-12 season
180. New Orleans Hornets
181. Boston Celtics
182. Klay Thompson
183. Scott Skiles
184. 8 times
185. 81 games
186. Golden State Warriors
187. Stephen Curry
188. Jerry west
189. Stephen Curry

190. 24 seconds
191. Kevin Durant
192. Rick Adelman
193. Los Angeles Lakers
194. Golden State Warriors
195. Los Angeles Lakers
196. 7 three-pointers
197. Baltimore bullets
198. Gar Heard
199. Warriors
200. Nikola Jokic
201. Detroit Pistons
202. Demar DeRozan
203. Orlando Magic
204. Stephen Curry
205. Goran Dragic
206. Heat
207. True
208. LeBron James
209. Anderson Varejao
210. JaVale McGee
211. Blake Griffin
212. Paul Pierce
213. The hood of a car
214. Kawhi Leonard
215. 2 points
216. Blake griffin
217. 48 minutes
218. New York Knicks
219. Danilo Gallinari
220. 2011
221. Oscar Robertson

222. LeBron James

223. Kobe Bryant

224. Knee injury

225. Magic Johnson

226. Creative writing

227. Kobe Bryant

228. George Gervin

229. Stephen Curry

230. Mike Fratello

231. Fort Wayne Zollner pistons

232. Allen Iverson

233. A Fox employee

234. Pat Riley

235. 6

236. Kobe Bryant

237. Sweden

238. 15 games

239. the Lakers

240. Boston Madison Square

241. Celtics

242. Mike D'antoni

243. The mascot of the Charlotte Hornets

244. Michael Jordan

245. A regulation period

246. Boogie

247. Philadelphia 76ers

248. Vancouver

249. Spain

250. Manchester

251. Glasgow

252. Newcastle

253. Leeds

254. Lakers
255. A head coach or a player on the court
256. 29
257. Possession is given to the opposing team
258. 94 feet by 50 feet
259. Backboard
260. Minnesota Timberwolves
261. Toni Kukoc
262. 55 boards
263. What's Up Doc
264. Ed Macauley
265. Larry Bird
266. Orlando Magic
267. 13
268. Penny Hardaway
269. An alley poop
270. 10
271. Expulsion from the game
272. Turnover
273. A run and gun
274. 1
275. Darko Milicic
276. Balance, eyes, elbow, follow through
277. Deflecting a pass
278. Technical foul
279. 3
280. NBA jam
281. Peach baskets
282. True
283. 3 seconds
284. UCLA
285. David Robinson

286. $5000

287. Stephen Curry

288. The Washington Bullets

289. Toronto Raptors

290. Vladimir Radmanovic

291. Merlin

292. 7

293. Reggie Harding

294. Toronto Raptors

295. Arch rivals

296. 2007

297. Cornbread

298. Boston Celtic

299. Michael Jordan

300. Dick Barnett

301. 2

302. Kareem Abdul-Jabbar

303. German

304. Flop

305. 4

306. Pacers

307. Raptors

308. Blue devils

309. Small ball

310. Sweden

311. A basket

312. Thunders

313. Nets

314. Bob Cousy

315. Blocking

316. Suns

317. 6

318. Italy
319. Walter
320. Pistons
321. Shooting guard
322. Staples center
323. Utah Jazz
324. High school
325. 30
326. White
327. Pistol Pete
328. Earvin
329. Mavericks
330. Bucks.
331. Alonzo Mourning
332. Timberwolves
333. Jazz
334. Olajuwon and Sampson
335. Pelicans
336. Spurs
337. 7
338. LeBron James
339. Heat
340. National
341. Court
342. Kings
343. Lithuania
344. Nikola Jokic
345. 41
346. Chicago Bulls
347. Andy Phillip
348. Boston Celtics
349. Chicago Bulls

350. Goaltending rule

351. Naismith Memorial Basketball

352. 0

353. 7

354. 8

355. 23

356. 13

357. 11

358. Canada

359. 6

360. Baseline

361. 120-107

362. Utah Jazz

363. East 13 - West 4

364. 0

365. Houston Rockets

366. No

367. Boston Celtics

368. Dallas Mavericks

369. Houston Rockets

370. Boston Celtics

371. NBA Jam

372. MVP

373. 0

374. Charlotte Bobcats

375. The Admiral

376. the Nationals

377. Yes

378. Chicago Bulls

379. The answer

380. Los Angeles Lakers

381. 2

382. 10

383. 28

384. 0

385. 23

386. Detroit Pistons

387. Philadelphia 76ers

388. 15

389. Forbes

390. Detroit Pistons

391. 26

392. Chicago Bulls

393. San Antonio Spurs

394. Indiana Pacers & Detroit Pistons

395. 1

396. 30

397. Philadelphia 76ers

398. 2

399. 1

400. Artis Gilmore

401. Minnesota Timberwolves

402. Phoenix Suns

403. Zaccharie Risacher

404. Lakers

405. Jerry West

406. Philadelphia, Pennsylvania

407. Dallas Mavericks

408. 1

409. 5

410. Houston

411. Miami

412. 0

413. Denver Nuggets

414. Coach

415. Charlotte

416. Dayton high school

417. Toronto Raptors

418. Dwayne Wade

419. True

420. San Antonio Spurs

421. Big Game James

422. 1st

423. 3

424. 9

425. 1

426. Yes

427. Lakers

428. Tony Parker

429. Memphis

430. New York Knicks

431. Michigan

432. Bounce it.

433. Little Caesars Arena

434. Footprint Center

435. True

436. Yes

437. Lower Merion

438. David Lee

439. 6

440. Golden State Warriors

441. Fort Wayne Zollner Pistons

442. Kobe Bryant

443. Bryant and O'Neal

444. Brooklyn Nets

445. Memphis

446. Dallas Mavericks

447. Real Madrid

448. The Greek Freak

449. 1

450. 1

451. Wilt Chamberlain

452. 726 games

453. Bill Russell

454. Yes

455. 11

456. True

457. True

458. It shall be started

459. At the time of the request

460. No

461. An official suspension of play

462. 1 point

463. The running score will be official

464. True

465. True

466. The opponent's score

467. 2 points

468. Two points

469. Three points

470. No

471. No

472. 8 ½ pounds

473. Crew chief

474. Replay center officials

475. Crew chief

476. LeBron James

477. The Charlotte Hornets

478. The Celtics

479. LeBron James

480. 10 players

481. JamesOn Curry

482. Washington Wizards

483. A snake

484. 73-9

485. NO

486. 43.4

487. 43.0

488. 43.6

489. Andrew Bynum

490. 3.9 seconds

491. Prigioni

492. New York Knicks

493. Golden State Warriors

494. 35 years

495. 7 feet 4 inches

496. 7 feet 3 inches

497. Bynum

498. Oliver Miller

499. Rasheed Wallace

500. Minneapolis Lakers

501. Michael Jordan

502. 22

503. 33

504. 1946

505. Muggsy Bogues

506. Father Knick

507. Yes

508. Yes

509. Bob Kurland

510. Vertical leap of 38 inches

511. Evan Ungar

512. Andre Drummond

513. Scott Skiles

514. Kareem Abdul

515. False, his highest is 7

516. True

517. 1990

518. Los Angeles Lakers

519. Yes

520. 907

521. 7,382

522. The Harlem Globetrotters

523. baseball

524. False

525. Utah Jazz

526. False

527. Toronto Huskies

528. Yes

529. Left hand

530. John Havlicek

531. Cleveland Cavaliers

532. 1996

533. Robert Parish

534. 28 years

535. Michael Jordan

536. 2011

537. 7382

538. John Stockton

539. 30 seconds

540. 12 minutes

541. 5 minutes

542. 15 minutes

543. Two minutes

544. Public address operator

545. Time expires

546. It is stopped

547. NO

548. 7

549. 4

550. 2

Basketball Word Search Puzzle

This word search puzzle is created around basketball terms and slangs, NBA teams, popular NBA Players and their nicknames, NBA coaches, and more . It is created to provide hours of fun searching for basketball lover, while they learn new words and facts.

HOW TO SOLVE

Find all the words listed below the word search grid on each page. Words are hidden in the grids of the puzzle in straight, unbroken lines: forward, backwards, up, down, diagonal top left to bottom right or diagonal bottom left to right.

Words can over lap and cross each other.

When you find a word, circle it in the grid and mark the word in the list so you will know it has been found. Each words should be searched for as individual word.

Solution to all the puzzles are at the last chapter of this book.

EASY TO CUT OUT

This book has wide inner margins, this will make it easy to cut out the page and take them with you as some people find this method convenient.

SPECIAL REQUEST

Please leave a brief honest review about this book on amazon.com. It will really be helpful. Thanks

Slang and Lingo 1

```
Q I T E D Q T Z C I Z F L S J O L E G A Q W
V Z Y C Q W D B U S P Z Y H H J N M W Y Z M
N T O I V N C U A F I V R B J O Z W I W D A
Q J Q O G N Z Z H C C C L L D K T S S N W Z
N Q L T N W H Z N N K L E N A K D C O O Z K
A M F S J T A E B K A C A F M Y O G L L P I
Y G U A G H E R P B N A O S D K U J A O W E
L X L G D R J A R W D N L U Y R B P T O C D
F B L H C E Y I C I R H Q N R G L A I K C K
U H C S Q E A S M M O H O B E T E H O P K G
L U O R K P L W I Y L U Q R V F D A N A F I
C P U U D O L S A I L X K U C R R L E S C J
E A R Y R I E C C Y B T A M R E I R I S Q X
H O T L K N Y L Y G L J K W O E B M L I V K
W R P I P T O A E Y W Z P T S T B Z L I Q H
D F R L U E O L A J M V Y U S H L P B E Q T
F I E D U R P Z B W D P P A O R E K V F H Z
B U S P I G W B Y W H V F U V O B J I U U Y
Z T S D E V H C I I F V P N E W H N Z T V M
W K X D J H M E G U T G T U R N O V E R V Q
X F N V W Y I F X O W C G U N H C Q M H Y O
C Q T W I C W N P Y A Z Q B Z D W X E Q N I
```

Airball	FullCourtPress	Screen
Alleyoop	Turnover	PickandRoll
Buzzer	NolookPass	Threepointer
Backcourt	Andone	ShotClock
DoubleDribble	Isolation	Layup
Fadeaway	Crossover	FreeThrow
Fastbreak		

92

Slang and Lingo 2

```
S X L M G W Z B K S K Y G F F K U B N Y U L
Z T N Z E N Z W G J L E L A Q Y N E I T E L
D W V V X E U C F J E J G X R Z L G S L B O
L B N C T E T V N F F P Z W W B R D H J F U
B A H U E D Z Z H Q I C X R U V I T D Z A M
G S E Z U H B U H D K B W O U K B G H O B O
U V G O X M C F B J J D D S J F N I V I A N
X C E S D F G G D G U E C I M P Y F K M P E
C H E V T Y T G R R L G C X F X H Q Z Q D Y
C I Q F Y Z G H X P O L Z T C W F S G S S S
G K T K Z O P B I E W Y D H O E E Y W Z P H
H J G L B G W R M M A B R M W R G S E I G O
Z R O X S F T I K W S A J A D U N K F E S T
C Q C V R C D C A S Q N M N J V M Z U Q M H
K Y C N H I X K L S X G A R B A G E T I M E
P M Q A G K A H X U R H W J L O L E A U O D
B I N T H E P A I N T U I I T T X A W Y L I
H H E C R U U N T O J C X C S Q H O O P S C
P F Z B L Y U D H C L F H U I J D N U K F N
O J E L O P S L P Y D P H N U O R U D T R Y
B L U P O S T E R I Z E D O J K Z Y K S C Y
D P T U W G F A T O A K A H V I H H W O O G
```

Brick	Clutch	PullUp
Swish	SixthMan	Hustle
Dime	Hoops	Handle
Posterized	GarbageTime	Bang
TripleDouble	BoxOut	MoneyShot
Dunkfest	Breakaway	InthePaint
HotHand		

93

Slang and Lingo 3

```
G C A T C H A N D S H O O T P O V A Y Y Q O
W Z Z S Z F R P S J C N J U M P S H O T R S
V E D K F L I S W F V X Y L T V A B G W A I
R P X Z K O K N S F X A K W N L J G I X L J
S P S F T A S I G P L B B O W Y E Q J W H I
U V C U V T C U D E A D B A L L S T S A O V
L J H O F E R N S R R I D Q W D L P P L O W
P Y J W W R E R G I H R N B Z E O K G A K C
D R O P S T E P P M P B O T Z X R K H Y S T
N J I V A V N N S E X A F L K G F X L W H S
W U N K E K A D Z T U S H A L A H E N Y O T
B O Q R F W S N D E F E N S E N K H N G T E
G J A A W R S E R R D L A H W W W O Q N O P
B U Z G O J I G I I R I P O S P J I J G W B
D W Q U G D S I V C A N N T B E R C O I Y A
M P I H R W T C E R I E H F Z O U R N P Z C
K T W U U Q Q D O W F E Z A M D G K W U Y K
P M Z N C Y W J N F V O O K S R V L E R Y R
E D A X N J U O F F E N S E W I J V S R K Y
U J R W U G P I B R P H V I U G F V G L I Z
Q P O B N F V A V X H T A C M V E L O V Y F
X C Z N O D P X K Y P U S C H S T K M A V S
```

Paint
Baseline
Perimeter
ShotFake
HookShot
Offense
Defense

Drive
OutletPass
DropStep
ScreenAssist
StepBack
CatchandShoot

ReverseLayup
DeadBall
FingerRoll
Floater
JumpShot

94

Slang and Lingo 4

```
X U C V A Y A W X Q S L N B B Q R R B K T A
Y S V N U V D Q C H D N F D U N A T C C P C
N J Z C T L Y B O R S E I X C D B E I R M C
H I Z W I X P U L H Z A W P K O H C R Y G R
Y P C B V U P Z K C B C F R E C B C C W O R
V G C Q B C N Y Z R R A O B T R N U U E B Y
X J S W A F M F G I I T D A S N M O S K E C
L F S W V Q P W C J C C E D B E S C S E F B
H D S E R Q Q U X E K H E J S P A G H K P M
Z B P L F D H U T L C A P V U X D R O I N E
D H L H G L X O U L I N T O C B Y E T G X Z
C T M R S A R P U Y T D H P O S T E R I Z E
W D W Y I P X T M L Y S R K F O I N O C R J
A B H A M J D F A W O H E S S E R L Q E U D
O M H I P D J M P X U O E P A P N I G B J Y
Y N R A I N M A K E R O Q D U Q Q G T P B L
S Y V C N T E P V P U T B A C K A H V W P B
A V Z Y Z D N M K F T N R Z E D N T O Q F N
O Z D K Z B L W F O K V S F U S P L A S H U
X A I D N R D E C E I J R F G W B P D Z C H
V M Q B T D T L S D R R A Z T T Z E M R V K
W Z B P J R Y R V S T C N Y L J H J K Y S Z
```

Rainmaker
Jelly
Sauce
Handles
GreenLight
Buckets
DeepThree

Splash
Dagger
CircusShot
Sniper
Putback
RimProtector

BrickCity
HeatCheck
Blowby
Posterize
CatchandShoot

95

Iconic Nicknames 1

```
O I K D D M O Q R C H A V G S Y L H C P P T
L D Y Q S V S Q G C T O X H C P F L A S H I
E G Q Q H B A Y G Y A E U H Y W W R C G E L
M K R V A L A N L X Z D P J D D W Y I Z E T
C Y S L B I G F U N D A M E N T A L W N V H
Z D X R G E Y D V T O U P I V A H M M J Z E
O L E U Z X S Y C N U Y V H R G F M X B Q W
U R U R F H J I D I E S E L I A C D B I G O
J I B L F C X Z J U I P X H U I L N I G G R
V Q A V T N K J D W M L N S G R F X R T G M
W L R T I P A C P W Y A I A V R O S D I Z E
N W O H O P Q Z Z Y M S M O N L S B M C C Y
X F A E R V O L Z U E H V B E O S O A K E S
N R B R P X C D H M J B Q B A N C K N E G G
T S S L I M R E A P E R R M Z Z W A A T A V
P T L L H J K J N U Y O A A K I M Z D W V A
T B J O O X G V S Z X T R S O E U A J R U I
I R Y J S N C H W M C H E F C U R R Y F G I
J R J D I D W H E Z L E A I E N D P H L T B
K G A K T O R U R F G R E E K F R E A K X R
B Y C C J R M P G H P K Y T S I H D D I B G
I F C Y F O V Z O Y G E F A J Y V W C S F L
```

Magic
BigO
DrJ
Diesel
Birdman
Iceman
BigTicket

ChefCurry
TheWorm
Answer
Mamba
Flash
BigFundamental

GreekFreak
KingJames
HumanHighlight
Admiral
SlimReaper
SplashBrother

96

Iconic Nicknames 2

```
A A O V P Z L H D D J G U M Z A V M P K B Y
B M Z P G P O U R E U T J E U W B W F P D J
B N H G Y A H X N W Y C J Z Z O L O G E J J
X N L Y P M L H F E U U N C L E D R E W Q K
L V R Z Y S J H T H E G L O V E K P P G W E
I I W Q Z F B I G S H O T R O B S E F H U M
V R N W P O S I T N S C A M T T F O H R Z P
W X B S U Q Q H G S Q M S W A L C Z W Z D P
D V J K A Z P U X P N E C L C C B H J I F Q
K X L A A N G I Y I A Z X B P C I W T C Z D
W Q F W H H I X A D M N N W N K G N D X J M
B S O D P B M T A E S S D B H B A G R A I G
M P K N Q D P C Y R O S L A I K R O K Y S T
K A R J K A A N H O T W P O Q G I K H F N B
H G R H C R A S H T H E B R O W S Y Y L O L
O E W P C M L I U H O H V Z Q Y T M F F A R
R N A P N M E K G E W M D H K V O M O G U Y
L T K G B L A C K J E S U S Y Q T K H O U B
C Z I M F W D B M E H G G K Z Z L K L J T F
Z E C H O C O L A T E T H U N D E R E M D H
R R M I T V Z U U B A G T U K B Y B Z J C V
D O O G W V Z B Y P L L C H Y P D M A D G R
```

BlackJesus	CaptainMarvel	Linsanity
ReignMan	ChocolateThunder	TheGlove
TheBrow	BigShotRob	TheJet
AgentZero	Zeke	Speedy
Spider	UncleDrew	Crash
BigAristotle	BigPanda	TMac
BigSmooth		

97

Iconic Nicknames 3

```
O T K Q C P V T G X I O R P N I R Q L A X L
Z C M B R Q H V R L B I G C O U N T R Y C W
Y X L I D Y C S R B M G I W J E G H O M A Z
N Z E Y N D U X O K Y O X O L F P E T L G J
K P Y T D Y L E Q Q S N J S I P S B C P 3 Y
D U J F I E A N H S M O R W Q I T E K A E C
K O F F C Z T D H W W P V P W S H A N C V K
B A J B Q A M H W N U A Z D J T O R F H J X
O H G F T R L D E Q Z U J O X O A D Y E D T
J Y F T G L J H W G T G H J P L D E G A D V
V P J F W V X S L M L B C K J P M X E L S V
A U V M V R X J Q F F I J Q W E D H T I D A
T I Y I T X V U Q V X X D R S T D C H I E F
M L C B Z D O L A R R Y L E G E N D E N Z M
H N F C L F G A S I R C H A R L E S M I X S
K X R A X R A A T B L S N G N A X F A U C J
A M F I L B G R I S J K I P W O I G I U Z B
O K A B L O M X L B O B I G Z K O N L Z S F
G L E R H L M B T L E Q U F Y D Q Q M H M O
E T N V Q K B H O H X S L K G N G Z A A M D
Z L F G I N A C T U G V M I C E M A N W N X
W L M J F F K P A C J S B I G B E N N K U P
```

BigBen
TheMailman
PistolPete
TheBigRedhead
KD
SirCharles
BigCountry

BigDog
Chief
LarryLegend
TheBeard
ClydetheGlide
TheClaw

BigZ
Hawk
RainMan
IceMan
Stilt
CP3

Iconic Nicknames 4

```
V I E Y A F U H A T R C O P R E Z X X T J P
Z A D B C S P O Y H Q I K S X U M K D N X I
H P A U M E C U R E L K B C Q U Y T A N W H
T B X X C M E S B H A M I G H T Y M O U S E
T H E I X U J M M A T G G N W B H H H J A I
O Z U X Y D I W K M A O C Q G C E T A N L N
F J K N E P O A B M I A A I T K U F Z I Y D
S H A Q D A D D Y E R T T U A R O B B S G M
H L S J Y E O A O R C G D O T T D N I J N T
U V I B Z N R M W W A G S E V A H G G U Y P
F F V M I D X D Y N N G H S E H V X S A U W
R U M F D M X D A I A T M U P V O Y H R H L
C E Q Q J U O H K N D B O Q V G T P O I V G
Q Z R A D P C N L H A L S W D I I B T J S B
J W Z H B D U K F G T R G O N Q E R B T Z W
P H G Z W D W Q D E V R W A Y F N B O H M Y
I O L K E Q A U E D K S S Z T O R Z B E H Q
T G S H T C T W F N F N V L K G O E H K T Q
U Q T H P G S P G O I N C O E W C W D I O W
J G E H I T V P J V X E U P K X K D Y D J Z
Y S R K D A E G Z E A Q J G P A A C M I I B
U R G I L L Z D F K F N X P E R V B H D M E
```

AirCanada	ThunderDan	SlimDuck
TheTruth	Juice	TheDunkingDutchman
SweetLou	MightyMouse	ShaqDaddy
DrayMagic	Vinsanity	DowntownFreddie
KingKong	BigCat	GOAT
Rock	TheKid	BigShotBob
TheHammer		

Coaches 1

```
B D O Z X Q M D N N B W P J O O V Z Q Q F J
R Y Q H Y I N I J E R R Y S L O A N U M T E
O D P H Q W H S J L A R R Y B R O W N N S Y
T O M T H I B O D E A U F P T L L S L R F N
F C T G K R M Q I P R E Q S F T P C U A D T
G R X Z R L E N N Y W I L K E N S N X D H S
R I C K C A R L I S L E K L J F K V I O F W
H V V O G R E G G P O P O V I C H K S N N E
Y E V A R N R A E P X T M Z I J N K Y N E E
H R N N E E W Y S R G A Y N G O C T L E U H
I S K E D W D K O W V L L X S L A W C L V R
Z J W K A H I H S Z A H B A W P N R N S U T
L Y P X U R O J O D H C J U O D S N K O C J
N Z W W E P B X K L G I E W P I O C D N A A
Z I E R R D A C C H Z F G H I R R G B W E C
Z P E O B X U T R B T M W E Y L P K I F G K
E C V G A H Y B G C L P A T R I L E Y R Q R
P H J Q C E M A P T Y O D N G R C H X H V A
N X W P H I L J A C K S O N A B N E A G P M
F Y I C D F C B U K G S T E V E K E R R A S
C K S M I P Z O O W D Z G Y U U O G V L D A
X W U Q K V L X E P I N B V K N D O S X E Y
```

GreggPopovich	PhilJackson	JackRamsay
ErikSpoelstra	ChuckDaly	DonNelson
SteveKerr	RedHolzman	TyronnLue
PatRiley	DocRivers	NickNurse
RedAuerbach	LarryBrown	WillHardy
LennyWilkens	RickCarlisle	TomThibodeau
JerrySloan	100	JasonKidd

Coaches 2

```
V N P T Y T Q E R U G E T V X K Y P T A M T
N I A L L H B J T S N H Z V V K C U O W O C
L V M J T E B Q O T R M I K E D A N T O N I
Z Z I X H F J A M A H L M O S L E Y N P T H
M M K P V Y J C S W T Z A C A W U E E D Y R
C M E Q R H R G L U Z B R M I K E B R O W N
O H B B N P E V U H C H K G N R T R U X I K
B N U O X W D U W G F T D Z G Q S F D F L E
A Z D B E O I S L M L F A E M N J C Y M L C
W L E O S J C Y U E W F I X I R O G T B I E
U L N V I O K W G V E L G K C I E C O X A D
F N H R N H I O S P L H N A H C M J M V M J
S A O U Q N V A A I C E E V A K A J J A S G
U X L X K K D W W T J D A Q E A Z J A Y A K
E S Z F N U B B I R L M U E L D Z P N W L X
G U E A B N L F O A R V L I M E U D O K A V
I S R W W D L L K Q U D T E A L L V V C T L
K F A X Y L Y N H P P Z O J L M L F I J T L
K X Q C I A I S W M U N P S O A A I C O L W
U K G B T I H I D L W J W O N N D L H N E C
W H Z N L L N Z S G E O R G E K A R L E S U
M Z Z Q M H G E K U E T F B W H Y A H S F T
```

JJRedick	MikeBudenholzer	GeorgeKarl
WillieGreen	MarkDaigneault	FrankVogel
MichaelMalone	JoeMazzulla	MikeDAntoni
MikeBrown	JamahlMosley	RudyTomjanovich
JohnKundla	TaylorJenkins	KCJones
MontyWilliams	AlAttles	RickAdelman
BillFitch		ImeUdoka

NBA Arenas

```
E  I  T  M  N  P  N  C  I  W  X  H  A  P  E  I  Y  Z  L  A  V  N
A  D  K  R  U  Q  E  L  S  E  E  D  R  G  I  E  C  A  I  B  K  Z
M  O  E  V  V  X  T  J  I  D  E  L  A  Y  F  M  J  J  D  N  V  A
X  B  R  X  S  K  U  X  Q  T  P  G  L  D  X  O  Z  W  O  M  N  G
J  E  I  N  X  P  K  M  I  G  T  N  R  S  I  Z  A  L  B  S  P  F
I  D  J  H  P  E  E  N  J  R  X  L  E  I  F  I  L  Q  L  T  P  Y
I  Y  X  V  X  D  U  C  O  Q  S  M  E  J  K  A  S  E  Y  A  E  H
L  D  H  G  H  P  B  M  T  I  U  J  R  C  B  T  R  F  E  T  Y  B
Z  H  D  F  G  Y  T  X  H  R  E  S  L  T  A  D  E  G  L  E  O  Q
U  E  A  E  A  C  R  O  W  U  S  O  A  R  E  D  F  O  F  H  P
T  T  X  V  K  E  J  F  O  E  X  M  I  R  C  O  S  M  W  A  C  N
W  L  X  C  X  V  X  A  Z  A  D  U  A  G  L  W  O  A  P  R  G  M
S  V  O  R  A  E  O  Z  S  G  I  H  E  E  A  C  B  P  R  M  H  R
Q  R  E  A  D  D  A  H  R  F  K  G  Q  T  Y  S  P  D  U  S  H  T
H  S  F  E  N  W  V  N  O  D  F  O  O  A  S  P  Q  Z  J  S  L  D
W  W  F  O  O  T  P  R  I  N  T  Y  P  L  G  F  A  P  H  T  Y  G
D  D  O  A  L  C  R  Y  P  T  O  C  O  M  T  W  C  E  T  I  M  P
W  B  C  P  U  H  H  G  A  T  D  G  A  R  D  E  N  D  Z  Y  K  I
B  N  E  Y  P  A  C  P  H  A  B  A  P  F  F  N  Q  H  J  N  J  W
J  M  A  D  I  S  O  N  S  Q  U  A  R  E  D  Y  Z  N  L  R  G  Z
D  P  Q  A  M  E  R  I  C  A  N  A  I  R  L  I  N  E  S  D  S  J
X  G  E  G  X  I  W  A  B  A  O  C  T  J  W  P  L  A  L  S  J  F
```

StateFarm
TDGarden
Barclays
Spectrum
United
RocketMortgage
AmericanAirlines

Ball
LittleCaesars
Chase
Toyota
Cryptocom
FedExForum

Kaseya
Target
MadisonSquare
Paycom
Kia
WellsFargo
Footprint

102

NBA Teams

```
J Y Y C B X U S K L U P P O J L D H N C O T
T S H P U T X V T S P I N Z B V C C F W T L
Q H I Z Q G P P I M O B K Q S F G U M D A V
O S C Z G A K K H E A K X N S Z I B A G U D
Q G D J B H X U U B Q V A Z I E A E T O H C
Y G V H L X R I Q W F C E U G C I S X E I O
S Y Y D P P G O L T I R V R P M K S E V C W
U Y S M K Y G X P L G J Q G I W W S V E E V
J D V Q G A W L E X C R V G A C S U B B L M
B J J V G O A P X I S A A H B E K N V M T V
Z K R J A N U G G E T S A F U O Y S E V I A
M H L Q W E H A P E E F M L L K J H P T C V
D Y Y F A S M J W I Q L V C L I P P E R S V
W B S A M V U A L A S P U R S N L Z F A C S
L C E V W Q G Z J R R T N B B G O X B H T J
X D J A L P Z Z E U V R O M G S S J R A J J
S K M W B I F K V Z E M I N R I U Z E D K O
L O W V R B A G W H I J P O S Y W R N S S V
N P L G H L S H K W Z G T Z R V H D I V G L
M N R D P O S W G B H P U V B S G J P U C D
W P L E H Q I N B L A Q B L B G F D K Z X P
V B I O F L X P X R O N S C P X B M V Z G F
```

Lakers	Spurs	Jazz
Celtics	Knicks	Hawks
Warriors	Raptors	Kings
Heat	Nuggets	Pistons
Bulls	Mavericks	Magic
Nets	Grizzlies	Suns
Clippers		Pelicans

103

NBA Team Cities

```
K M Y L X Y M I P G N C A A J O I V M E P Q
Y X F G P L Y J Q W N E I M B C Q E N U H G
U D E L F R Y F P S A I W Z N T I N H R I W
M Z D S S T U O Y G Y D I O R A X V V S L T
A Y N T T X W E J S T O T K R T I N L Q A I
H R L M R L D A Y R O S R L Q L B Y O N D U
O R Y Y F J U W P K O V F A R A E P S Q E R
I P D J G B O V N B V C J H E N O A A H L U
F U U V S K C I C H A R L O T T E R N Q P C
B I U G B X A B H M U E T M N A M C G S H X
C L K H L R A C R C H I C A G O A Z E X I U
U Y Y N V S Q Y N O O N D C S S O A L N A L
E G V A B G H T P R O Y A I O R A G E Y C Y
H U J G C B J K T H Y K L T R Y L O S X O P
P T W G Z N R E R U O O L Y L H H A Y R N B
I A V U M O D E S W P U A Y A P O F X E T J
C W X B Y P V M I A M I S J N T E Z F V U G
K H R W H N W S E T B S I T D C E Z E R A K
C L E V E L A N D V R M Q L O X J Z I H U W
I N V D A A N F H P W Y A L A N H J O U W Q
E B I N D I A N A P O L I S D P J D H Q Z J
I I O K M Z E J N C E T X C E M U F M I B J
```

Atlanta
Boston
Brooklyn
Charlotte
Chicago
Cleveland
Dallas

Denver
Detroit
Houston
Indianapolis
LosAngeles
Miami

Minneapolis
NewOrleans
NewYork
OklahomaCity
Orlando
Philadelphia
Phoenix

104

NBA Events 1

```
X V S R N F R X Z I Z X W R Y L Y W E H S Z
W S E E T L Z L K X X Z O I H Y V M H A D S
R X E X R Y F S T S F H U S I K A D N M U U
R M P L C Y F I H K Q N D I J W G P G F U A
H S B N G F C O N F E R E N C E S S E P C R
E K G S O U H U Z A M G L G G L B W M B Z K
H I C Y U G D P V K L O T S D I V E I M F T
H L A H L M V P T K V S A T G T C E K S V K
K L L A A D M A E H Z D H A Q E F T Z C J E
P S L L O M Y E B B N L L R V E N S U T Y A
M C S Q R B P S R U I X N S U I L I M A N P
C H T Q B N Y I O L Z C B L O G R X A B Q M
I A A A Y G Z R O Q E Z R P B H D T R N N P
X L R P H I T L H N Y A E E A T I E C Y U K
I L W Q X S O U P B S E G R P J H E H Y G U
U E J L R M P D L P R H I U B V S N M Z J D
L N L I A C E W R H U A I D E E O S A Y O I
F G F Z D R A F T K F M D P U O A V D J R Z
S E N V E O L M P D J F T K D A I T N H Y W
F W G D V I U W Z R X F S N X Y H F E Y A H
M Z F V U Q U J C L G X N L C M J Z S R W T
O M Y G E M G N E T I P O F F T D I S X O T
```

Draft	Championship	MarchMadness
Finals	Conference	EliteEight
AllStar	TipOff	SweetSixteen
Playoffs	BuzzerBeater	FirstRound
SlamDunk	MVP	SummerLeague
SkillsChallenge	ThreePoint	
RisingStars		

105

NBA Events 2

```
S E M I F I N A L S T E A M P R A C T I C E
C J Q S M X Z F U I P U H V L D C M R I I L
D L U D T M W S F C P G O Y C R A D A A O D
D T Y O B O T D F Q X K G T T A Y I D R O M
Y A B G Z R T I G I T K B Y F F F V E R F W
T P A J Q B C I S J N V Z L M T K I D O P D
B N Y W P R O O K I E S H O W C A S E I F L
N U M P L A Y I N G A M E G I O V I A L A E
O B T L A V V X D F X R K P E M R O D Z J A
V K J A Y I Y M J R E C Y D D B G N L R Z G
K J N Y I O T E V M A R G I Y I T F I E G U
Q Q R E N R M R R I E F E H X N Y I N G K E
C L E R T H J C A T Y L T N Y E M N E U V S
K N K A O C G J T I F S B P C W Q A C L R T
H V R W U G P O M U N Z B M A E Z L K A D A
Z N D A R E L J N V T I U G E R F S H R J N
K Z B R N O P E N I N G N I G H T I E S X D
N M I D A M A N A K I Y D G N T Y Y N E N I
A Z G S M V B O R G I V J X C B R K G A B N
V X W O E L Y U N N U M E D I A D A Y S L G
P T B P N S F A I Q H E K D D A M Q F O F S
Q Y O Z T W A C W H Q W J C B F T P I N L U
```

RegularSeason
OpeningNight
TradeDeadline
PlayinTournament
DivisionFinals
LeagueStandings
Semifinals

MediaDay
DraftCombine
RookieShowcase
TeamPractice
TrainingCamp
GLeague

ConferenceFinals
PlayerAwards
PlayinGame
LotteryPick
DraftParty

Basketball Gear 1

```
U R W Q X Z I D I W H N D Q Y B H O N C M J
W R Z T H P K X F L I X D H U F L H F W T E
F S E W G S B V O W N T U B N L U E Q Q K L
Y N F D K Y P A J E V W H I F W T D A R L B
W E H G T W B R S O B A C K B O A R D E W O
P A W A B U Q V Y O C L H C A A M R J B A W
J K T R M M V D U H T S J K Q B L D M O L P
S E K E G S N K M E U B Q M G E B L P U E A
E R R F R A H M B K A F B B V P G J L N P D
G S F S B B T W C K M O U T H G U A R D R S
S X S D E H O O P K Q Z F G P W Z O P E F E
N E A H F Y L T R I P C L N I R O X X R K Q
J E H K O C T K T A W H U O I G U K J C M G
H W J C T R V G B L D W G I G F O S C B I V
Z R C O U R T M R E E V V I G J Q A J H A
E I H G E I H S O V P J I L D L E Q S B M G
X S Z L W M K I L N U O W K W X B F B I O U
M T N G P S D G B K R R O H E T L H P H W W
W B A A A M Y P F J Y P K N R U K T W S D H
A A W C A P F C L T Q T M R X M M F C F R V
A N S C D U M Z B O S P S P W E Y A X S M T
Q D I V Y W U H Y O U M L L A D A W V T D K
```

Jersey
Sneakers
Backboard
Ball
Hoop
Net
Wristband

Headband
Court
Rims
Warmups
Mouthguard
Shorts

ElbowPads
ShotClock
Rebounder
WaterBottle
Gatorade

107

Basketball Gear 2

```
X P M N O S R G F R P L W Z N V I L S Z J C
V R C L P C A Z S H O O T E R S L E E V E Q
E D W I S Y V T C H M I R M H W A H R I K R
R C I M I U U T U L C A N K L E B R A C E E
C O P P F G A B L H A R V W M A S L D M V B
K M R J K W W A R M U P P A N T S R B E E X
U P A P P H Y V R N N Y E T K T A Q E E X C
L R C O L V S H A N O E Y A X O E L Z H K K
J E T R A I N E R K I T J P B W S A Y F U Q
Z S I C P Q M P D W S C C E G E P Z M Z X O
J S C W X H M B R C Z Y R R E L G D N H U A
S I E Z C M M A J A G O C N U X D Q W C A W
Q O J J H K F N S V C A K B I N U O W C R T
Y N E G Z C O N E S J T X C J H F N N N O I
G S R B Z R A F A C A H I I Y T F Z Z A Q Q
O H S X P G M O D O X G G C Y A E N J W U X
Y O E M T Z R I W J W A E K E Q L H G J Y B
T R Y Q Y P O X I T D N B G K B B G Z P X L
E T V B M C L I P B O A R D U G A Q I S O T
G S E N G R L W A Y T T Y E Z N G L P T Q M
G L C R E F E R E E W H I S T L E W L K M E
D K I L U C R I F B E C O Q G K O G B V E N
```

Stopwatch
Scoreboard
Clipboard
PracticeJersey
RefereeWhistle
Cones
PracticeBall

DuffelBag
AnkleBrace
KneeSleeve
WarmupPants
ShooterSleeve
TeamHat

CompressionShorts
FoamRoller
MassageGun
Tape
SweatTowel
TrainerKit

108

Rules of the Game 1

```
J U M P B A L L D Q L L A O A S W Z B B E D
K N G G P I J J Q A G A Q W T V N X E H A X
B S M S M K T K I R H H P P N B O I D T M K
F P M Q F L K R G X J B O W F L A G R A N T
T O E F J T N D X P Z I S J Y S B J E R G E
U R L W U L L H G B T N S M Z P L T O K H S
U T U A V C V F E H G T E J I O E Q E H F K
W S J U X H M H B E C M S J T L G N E Q I C
Z M M K C A R R Y I N G S T B N Q B P G V D
A A N S L R Y W U I Z A I U I S A M U H E N
B N Y Q T G T V N T T O O D O S G P L D S T
N L U U U I N B O U N D N O T L T A I T E D
P I O O L N M M O Q P E E E E X C V Z H C V
L K Q C H G Z E A E T F O U L I I S B U O G
X E F Y K A M W T L P E W P N D H C G C N C
O V E R T I M E A Q L N Z H W S U M Z D D D
D U I O T U N O X M Q S C G O K R D I D R F
D S S D O B G G W Y P E R S O N A L F O U L
O X T F C L K G V X T R A V E L I N G S L Z
G H V G U L Z N R Z I Q S M R U G Z P C E Y
K A X E S H O T C L O C K V I O L A T I O N
H O U E D V G Q E Y V W M J D C I G O P C N
```

Foul	Charging	Unsportsmanlike
Technical	Traveling	Inbound
Possession	Goaltending	Defense
Overtime	ShotClockViolation	Zone
Timeout	PersonalFoul	DoubleTeam
JumpBall	Flagrant	Carrying
Blocking		FivesecondRule

109

Rules of the Game 2

```
V K I Z U L J J L K H T S H S E M A L T V Y M
I D L Y H Z H C M V C C U Z N J J K D D B H
D U C Q I W L C E L O O S E B A L L F O U L
B E L T R A V E L I N G R Y I C E O V U E J
D H F V G O A L T E N D I N G X P E X B E Z
R C I E S X A F F L A G R A N T F O U L B O
A U P L N B N F I X S H O T C L O C K E L L
K K E M P S X I V U N E F G T X A Y E T O A
E Z G M C N I Z E C S Z F B D N E T G E C S
W Y U A J J N V S N E A E K H R W O B A K Y
Z J F N P W T P E R S O N A L F O U L M I D
L M G T D K M F C T H L S D J J E B H N N X
Z Q P O R V E D O O H Z I L R K A A B U G X
Y H A M U D G Q N V Z R V X F T X B O Y F M
V H O A E B Z O D A F X E H C X H B R S O C
G K B N L L W A S M G H R E A E N Q S L U C
G N O A Y V D D O U B L E D R I B B L E L M
Z Z B J X C C N J I D G B V R Y J V P M Q U
U H U V X I T V A K G S O X Y Y T K Z C N U
Y C L E A R P A T H F O U L Z X Y A K W N S
L X N I B I 2 4 S E C O N D C L O C K F F G
L P T H R E E S E C O N D S J G M Y C L J W
```

PersonalFoul
DoubleTeam
ClearPathFoul
Traveling
Carry
ZoneDefense
MantoMan

ThreeSeconds
DefensiveThree
DoubleDribble
JumpBall
24SecondClock
FiveSeconds

FlagrantFoul
Inbound
LooseBallFoul
GoalTending
ShotClock
BlockingFoul
OffensiveRebound

Popular NBA Player

```
B F K M E I K W G A V A A H Y O C R K U Y H
S A Z A O B U P G Y Z L X D M V Q U B D X B
L P B Y I I E I Y G F I M G H F G S R U Y F
A F K H X R J P M B L W V D S W N S F R Q W
Q I I A J D G P A U S U B H O Y I E M A Y T
D I R K E R U E G X O P P N W M D L B N O P
B I V E R S O N I N B G E S A R Q L T T P Y
W W R E L I K B C J Q D V D Z D Q L U Z P B
A D E M H S H A Q A R U R S F T V O N G V D
F V A W K J O R D A N E G L D N G K P Y W P
L T K Q A O P K H L U P C A T D R O C H W D
A K Q U R C B L U K A L U P A Q A K B T I E
J U D Q E G R E E K G Y V L D T P K Z O L Y
L Y Q Q E Z W Y A B L D O R Z S Z U N E H E
G X I A M K W G A Q R V L F I A W Q V X F S
D D T F F H R G W L I O G N K D V H N P L O
T K Z F E A X O V I E X N H L D A M S D S T
Q J O I O A C F O C F A L Q Y T E N A F J C
K O H K Y Y Z V V V I M S V D A K X Q Z V J
H F Z M R M K W Y G R X J Q F V H X Q B C J
S H S S V V T T Q K F O T D I I Y H L P Z W
E O J F X E D A Z X S Z O Y G T V R Q C I G
```

Jordan	Magic	Duncan
LeBron	Bird	Dirk
Kobe	Kareem	Barkley
Shaq	Hakeem	Pippen
Curry	Iverson	Russell
Durant	Giannis	Harden
Wilt		Luka

111

Slang and Lingo 1

```
Q I T E D Q T Z C I Z F L S J O L E G A Q W
V Z Y C Q W D B U S P Z Y H H J N M W Y Z M
N T O I V N C U A F I V R B J O Z W I W D A
Q J Q O G N Z Z H C C C L D K T S S N W Z
N Q L T N W H Z N N K L E N A K D C O O Z K
A M F S J T A E B K A C A F M Y O G L L P I
Y G U A G H E R P B N A O S D K U J A O W E
L X L G D R J A R W D N L U Y R B P T O C D
F B L H C E Y I C I R H Q N R G L A I K C K
U H C S Q E A S M M O H O B E T E H O P K G
L U O R K P L W I Y L U Q R V F D A N A F I
C P U U D O L S A I L X K U C R R L E S C J
E A R Y R I E C C Y B T A M R E I R I S Q X
H O T L K N Y L Y G L J K W O E B M L I V K
W R P I P T O A E Y W Z P T S T B Z L I Q H
D F R L U E O L A J M V Y U S H L P B E Q T
F I E D U R P Z B W D P P A O R E K V F H Z
B U S P I G W B Y W H V F U V O B J I U U Y
Z T S D E V H C I I F V P N E W H N Z T V M
W K X D J H M E G U T G T U R N O V E R V Q
X F N V W Y I F X O W C G U N H C Q M H Y O
C Q T W I C W N P Y A Z Q B Z D W X E Q N I
```

Slang and Lingo 2

```
S X L M G W Z B K S K Y G F F K U B N Y U L
Z T N Z E N Z W G J L E L A Q Y N E I T E L
D W V V X E U C F J E J G X R Z L G S L B O
L B N C T E T V N F F P Z W W B R D H J F U
B A H U E D Z Z H Q I C X R U V I T D Z A M
G S E Z U H B U H D K B W O U K B G H O B O
U V G O X M C F B J J D S J F N I V I A N
X C E S D F G G D G U E C I M P Y F K M P E
C H E V T Y T G R R L G C X F X H Q Z Q D Y
C I Q F Y Z G H X P O L Z T C W F S G S S S
G K T K Z O P B I E W Y D H O E E Y W Z P H
H J G L B G W R M M A B R M W R G S E I G O
Z R O X S F T I K W S A J A D U N K F E S T
C Q C V R C D C A S Q N M N J V M Z U Q M H
K Y C N H I X K L S X G A R B A G E T I M E
P M Q A G K A H X U R H W J L O L E A U O D
B I N T H E P A I N T U I I T T X A W Y L I
H H E C R U U N T O J C X C S Q H O O P S C
P F Z B L Y U D H C L F H U I J D N U K F N
O J E L O P S L P Y D P H N U O R U D T R Y
B L U P O S T E R I Z E D O J K Z Y K S C Y
D P T U W G F A T O A K A H V I H H W O O G
```

Slang and Lingo 3

```
G C A T C H A N D S H O O T P O V A Y Y Q O
W Z Z S Z F R P S J C N J U M P S H O T R S
V E D K F L I S W F V X Y L T V A B G W A I
R P X Z K O K N S F X A K W N L J G I X L J
S P S F T A S I G P L B B O W Y E Q J W H I
U V C U V T C U D E A D B A L L S T S A O V
L J H O F E R N S R R I D Q W D L P P L O W
P Y J W W R E R G I H R N B Z E O K G A K C
D R O P S T E P P M P B O T Z X R K H Y S T
N J I V A V N N S E X A F L K G F X L W H S
W U N K E K A D Z T U S H A L A H E N Y O T
B O Q R F W S N D E F E N S E N K H N G T E
G J A A W R S E R R D L A H W W W O Q N O P
B U Z G O J I G I I R I P O S P J I J G W B
D W Q U G D S I V C A N N T B E R C O I Y A
M P I H R W T C E R I E H F Z O U R N P Z C
K T W U U Q Q D O W F E Z A M D G K W U Y K
P M Z N C Y W J N F V O O K S R V L E R Y R
E D A X N J U O F F E N S E W I J V S R K Y
U J R W U G P I B R P H V I U G F V G L I Z
Q P O B N F V A V X H T A C M V E L O V Y F
X C Z N O D P X K Y P U S C H S T K M A V S
```

Slang and Lingo 4

```
X U C V A Y A W X Q S L N B B Q R R B K T A
Y S V N U V D Q C H D N F D U N A T C C P C
N J Z C T L Y B O R S E I X C D B E I R M C
H I Z W I X P U L H Z A W P K O H C R Y G R
Y P C B V U P Z K C B C F R E C B C C W O R
V G C Q B C N Y Z R R A O B T R N U U E B Y
X J S W A F M F G I I T D A S N M O S K E C
L F S W V Q P W C J C C E D B E S C S E F B
H D S E R Q Q U X E K H E J S P A G H K P M
Z B P L F D H U T L C A P V U X D R O I N E
D H L H G L X O U L I N T O C B Y E T G X G
C T M R S A R P U Y T D H P O S T E R I Z E
W D W Y I P X T M L Y S R K F O I N O C R J
A B H A M J D F A W O H E S S E R L Q E U D
O M H I P D J M P X U O E P A P N I G B J Y
Y N R A I N M A K E R O Q D U Q Q G T P B L
S Y V C N T E P V P U T B A C K A H V W P B
A V Z Y Z D N M K F T N R Z E D N T O Q F N
O Z D K Z B L W F O K V S F U S P L A S H U
X A I D N R D E C E I J R F G W B P D Z C H
V M Q B T D T L S D R R A Z T T Z E M R V K
W Z B P J R Y R V S T C N Y L J H J K Y S Z
```

Iconic Nicknames 1

Iconic Nicknames 2

Iconic Nicknames 3

Iconic Nicknames 4

Coaches 1

```
B D O Z X Q M D N N B W P J O O V Z Q Q F J
R Y Q H Y I N I J E R R Y S L O A N U M T E
O D P H Q W H S J L A R R Y B R O W N N S Y
T O M T H I B O D E A U F P T L L S L R F N
F C T G K R M Q I P R E Q S F T P C U A D T
G R X Z R L E N N Y W I L K E N S N X D H S
R I C K C A R L I S L E K L J F K V I O F W
H V V O G R E G G P O P O V I C H K S N N E
Y E V A R N R A E P X T M Z I J N K Y N E E
H R N N E E W Y S R G A Y N G O C T L E U H
I S K E D W D K O W V L L X S L A W C L V R
Z J W K A H I H S Z A H B A W P N R N S U T
L Y P X U R O J O D H C J U O D S N K O C J
N Z W W E P B X K L G I E W P I O C D N A A
Z I E R R D A C C H Z F G H I R R G B W E C
Z P E O B X U T R B T M W E Y L P K I F G K
E C V G A H Y B G C L P A T R I L E Y R Q R
P H J Q C E M A P T Y O D N G R C H X H V A
N X W P H I L J A C K S O N A B N E A G P M
F Y I C D F C B U K G S T E V E K E R R A S
C K S M I P Z O O W D Z G Y U U O G V L D A
X W U Q K V L X E P I N B V K N D O S X E Y
```

Coaches 2

```
V N P T Y T Q E R U G E T V X K Y P T A M T
N I A L L H B J T S N H Z V V K C U O W O C
L V M J T E B Q O T R M I K E D A N T O N I
Z Z I X H F J A M A H L M O S L E Y N P T H
M M K P V V J C S W T Z A C A W U E E D Y R
C M E Q R H R G L U Z B R M I K E B R O W N
O H B B N P E V U H C H K G N R T R U X I K
B N U O X W D U W G F T D Z G Q S F D F L E
A Z D B E O I S L M L F A E M N J C Y M L C
W L E O S J C Y U E W F I X I R O G T B I E
U L N V I O K W G V E L G K C I E C O X A D
F N H R N H I O S P L H N A H C M J M V M J
S A O U Q N V A A I C E E V A K A J J A S G
U X L X K K D W W T J D A Q E A Z J A Y A K
E S Z F N U B B I R L M U E L D Z P N W L X
G U E A B N L F O A R V L I M E U D O K A V
I S R W W D L L K Q U D T E A L L V V C T L
K F A X Y L Y N H P P Z O J L M L F I J T L
K X Q C I A I S W M U N P S O A A I C O L W
U K G B T I H I D L W J W O N N D L H N E C
W H Z N L L N Z S G E O R G E K A R L E S U
M Z Z Q M H G E K U E T F B W H Y A H S F T
```

NBA Arenas

```
E I T M N P N C I W X H A P E I Y Z L A V N
A D K R U Q E L S E E D R G I E C A I B K Z
M O E V V X T J I D E L A Y F M J J D N V A
X B R X S K U X Q T P G L D X O Z W O M N G
J E I N X P K M I G T N R S I Z A L B S P F
I D J H P E E N J R X L E I F X L Q L T P Y
I Y X V X D U C O Q S M E J K A S E Y A E H
L D H G H P B M T I U J R C B T R F E T Y B
Z H D F G Y T X H R E S L T A D E G L E O Q
U E A E A E C R O W U S O A R E D F O F H P
T T X V E J F O E X M I R C O S M W A C N
W L X C X V X A Z A D U A G L W O A P R G M
S V O R A E O Z S G I H E E A C B P R M H R
Q R E A D D A H R F K G Q T Y S P D U S H T
H S F E N W V N O D F O O A S P Q Z J S L D
W W F O O T P R I N T Y P L G F A P H T Y G
D D O A L C R Y P T O C O M T W C E T I M P
W B C P U H H G A T D G A R D E N D Z Y K I
B N E Y P A C P H A B A P F F N Q H J N J W
J M A D I S O N S Q U A R E D Y Z N L R G Z
D P Q A M E R I C A N A I R L I N E S D S J
X G E G X I W A B A O C T J W P L A L S J F
```

NBA Teams

```
J Y Y C B X U S K L U P P O J L D H N C O T
T S H P U T X V T S P I N Z B V C C F W T L
Q H I Z Q G P P I M O B K Q S F G U M D A V
O S C Z G A K K H E A K X N S Z I B A G U D
Q G D J B H X U U B Q V A Z I E A E T O H C
Y G V H L X R I Q W F C E U G C I S X E I O
S Y Y D P P G O L T I R V R P M K S E V C W
U Y S M K Y G X P L G J Q G I W W S V E E V
J D V Q G A W L E X C R V G A C S U B B L M
B J J V G O A P X I S A A H B E K N V M T V
Z K R J A N U G G E T S A F U O Y S E V I A
M H L Q W E H A P E E F M L L K J H P T C V
D Y Y F A S M J W I Q L V C L I P P E R S V
W B S A M V U A L A S P U R S N L Z F A C S
L C E V W Q G Z J R R T N B B G O X B H T J
X D J A L P Z Z E U V R O M G S S J R A J J
S K M W B F K V Z E M I N R I U Z E D K O
L O W V R B A G W H I J P O S Y W R N S S V
N P L G H L S H K W Z G 7 R V H D I V G L
M N R D P O S W G B H P U V B S G J P U C D
V B I O F L X P X R O N S C P X B M V Z G F
```

114

NBA Team Cities

NBA Events 1

NBA Events 2

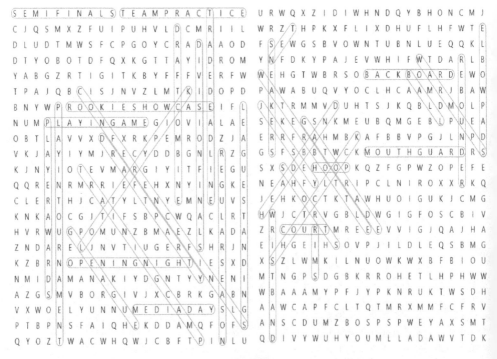

Basketball Gear 1

115

Basketball Gear 2

```
X P M N O S R G F R P L W Z N V I L S Z J C
V R C L P C A Z S H O O T E R S L E E V E Q
E D W I S Y V T C H M I R M H W A H R I K R
R C I M I U U T U L C A N K L E B R A C E E
C O P P F G A B L H A R V W M A S L D M V B
K M R J K W W A R M U P P A N T S R B E E X
U P A P P H Y V R N N Y E T K T A Q E E X C
L R C O L V S H A N O E Y A X O E L Z H K K
J E T R A I N E R K I T J P B W S A Y F U Q
Z S I C P Q M P D W S C C E G E P Z M Z X O
J S C W X H M B R C Z Y R R E L G D N H U A
S I E Z C M M A J A G O C N U X D Q W C A W
Q O J J H K F N S V C A K B I N U O W C R T
Y N E G Z C O N E S J T X C J H F N N N O I
G S R B Z R A F A C A H I I Y T F Z Z A Q Q
O H S X P G M O D O X G G C Y A E N J W U X
Y O E M T Z R I W J W A E K E Q L H G J Y B
T R Y Q Y P O X I T D N B G K B B G Z P X L
E T V B M C L I P B O A R D U G A Q I S O T
G S E N G R L W A Y T T Y E Z N G L P T Q M
G L C R E F E R E E W H I S T L E W L K M E
D K I L U C R I F B E C O Q G K O G B V E N
```

Rules of the Game 1

```
J U M P B A L L D Q L L A O A S W Z B B E D
K N G G P I J J Q A G A Q W T V N X E H A X
B S M S M K T K I R H H P P N B O I D T M K
F P M Q F L K R G X J B O W F L A G R A N T
T O E F J T N D X P Z I S J Y S B J E R G E
U R L W U L L H G B T N S M Z P L T O K H S
U T U A V C V F E H G T E J I O E Q E H F K
W S J U X H M H B E C M S J T L G N E Q I C
Z M M K C A R R Y I N G S T B N Q B P G V D
A A N S L R Y W U I Z A I U I S A M U H E N
B N Y Q T G T V N T T O O D O S G P L D S T
N L U U U I N B O U N D N O T L T A I T E D
P I O O L N M M O Q P E E E X C V Z H C V
L K Q C H G Z E A E T F O U L I I S B U O G
X E F Y K A M W T L P E W P N D H C G C N C
O V E R T I M E A Q L N Z H W S U M Z D D D
D U I O T U N O X M Q S C G O K R D I D R F
D S S D O B G G W Y P E R S O N A L F O U L
O X T F C L K G V X T R A V E L I N G S L Z
G H V G U L Z N R Z I Q S M R U G Z P C E Y
K A X E S H O T C L O C K V I O L A T I O N
H O U E D V G Q E Y V W M J D C I G O P C N
```

Rules of the Game 2

```
V K I Z U L J L K H T S H S E M A L T V Y M
I D L Y H Z H C M V C C U Z N J J K D D B H
D U C Q I W L C E L O O S E B A L L F O U L
B E L T R A V E L I N G R Y I C E O V U E J
D H F V G O A L T E N D I N G X P E X B E Z
R C I E S X A F F L A G R A N T F O U L B O
A U P L N B N F I X S H O T C L O C K E L L
K K E M P S X I V U N E F G T X A Y E T O A
E Z G M C N I Z E C S Z F B D N E T G E C S
W Y U A J J N V S N E A E K H R W O B A K Y
Z J F N P W T P E R S O N A L F O U L M I D
L M G T D K M F C T H L S D J J E B H N N X
Z Q P O R V E D O O H Z I L R K A A B U G X
Y H A M U D G Q N V Z R V X F T X B O Y F M
V H O A E B Z O D A F X E H C X H B R S O C
G K B N L L W A S M G H R E A E N Q S L U C
G N O A Y V D D O U B L E D R I B B L E L M
Z Z B J X C C N J I D G B V R J J V P M Q U
U H U V X I T V A K G S O X Y Y T K Z C N U
Y C L E A R P A T H F O U L Z X Y A K W N S
L X N I B I 2 4 S E C O N D C L O C K F F G
L P T H R E E S E C O N D S J G M Y C L J W
```

Popular NBA Player

```
B F K M E I K W G A V A A H Y O C R K U Y H
S A Z A O B U P G Y Z L X D M V Q U B D X B
L P B Y I I E I Y G F I M G H F G S R U Y F
A F K H X R J P M B L W V D S W N S F R Q W
Q I I A J D G P A U S U B H O Y I E M A Y T
D I R K E R U E G X O P P N W M D L B N O P
B I V E R S O N I N B G E S A R Q L T T P Y
W W R E L I K B C J Q D V D Z D Q L U Z P B
A D E M H S H A Q A R U R S F T V O N G V D
F V A W K J O R D A N E G L D N G K P Y W P
L T K Q A O P K H L U P C A T D R O C H W D
A K Q U R C B L U K A L U P A Q A K B T I E
J U D Q E G R E E K G Y V L D T P K Z O L Y
L Y Q Q E Z W Y A B L D O R Z S Z U N E H E
G X I A M K W G A Q R V L F I A W Q V X F S
D D T F F H R G W L I O G N K D V H N P L O
T K Z F E A X O V I E X N H L D A M S D S T
Q J O I O A C F O C F A L Q Y T E N A F J C
K O H K Y Y Z V V V I M S V D A K X Q Z V J
H F Z M R M K W Y G R X J Q F V H X Q B C J
S H S S V V T T Q K F O T D I I Y H L P Z W
E O J F X E D A Z X S Z O Y G T V R Q C I G
```

116

Made in the USA
Monee, IL
22 December 2024

74994261R00069